THE SIX WAYS OF ATHEISM
Six new or improved logical disproofs of the existence of God originated and put forward by Geoffrey Berg, a graduate of the University of Cambridge, England.

The author acknowledges assistance and helpful advice from Jane Bowler, Sanal Edamaruku, Janis Entwisle and Carl Pinel.

British Library Cataloguing in Publication Data
A catalogue record for this book is available from the British Library

ISBN: 978-0-9543956-6-7

Points concerning the content of this book may be emailed to: 'responsestothesixwaysofatheism@ymail.com'

Further copies of this book can be ordered from good bookshops or by logging onto 'www.thesixwaysofatheism.com' for single, multiple and trade orders.

In case of difficulty telephone 0044 845 3032750 (from outside the United Kingdom) or from 0845 303 2750 (from United Kingdom) during office hours of the United Kingdom.

THE SIX WAYS
OF ATHEISM

Geoffrey Berg

New Logical Disproofs Of The Existence of God

Six Improved Arguments for Atheism

Contents

Introduction

This is a collection of six different new valid arguments against belief in a monotheistic God. The arguments are original at least in some of their elements in each case. There are two arguments (The Man And God Comprehension Gulf Argument and The God Has No Explanatory Value Argument) why we humans should not believe in the existence of God. There is an argument (The Aggregate Of Qualities Argument) that in terms of statistical significance is equivalent to a disproof of the existence of God. There are also three complete and absolute disproofs of the existence of God (This Is Not The Best Possible World Argument, The Universal Uncertainty Argument and the Some Of God's Essential Qualities Cannot Exist Argument).

Some of these arguments are really as far as I know absolutely and completely original to myself. This applies to The Universal Uncertainty Argument and The Aggregate Of Qualities Argument. Some other arguments I have tweaked a lot. This applies to the Some Of God's Essential Qualities Cannot Exist Argument (which was a line of argumentation developed by Carneades and written down by Sextus Empiricus, although my main application to the purpose of life is, I think, original to myself). I have also considerably tweaked the This Is Not The Best Possible World Argument (which derives originally from the traditional argument based on suffering or evil in the world but which I have reworked and reformulated radically to prevent theists from evading it). I have merely tweaked the two other arguments a little in comparative terms. The Man And God Comprehension Gulf Argument is basically similar to an argument David Hume mentioned (without specifically endorsing it) in his Dialogues Concerning Natural Religion. However I think I have expressed it rather better and transformed it into logical paradoxes that clearly demonstrate the illogicality of human belief in God. The God Has No Explanatory Value Argument was in its original form a populist argument (i.e. if God created the world, who created God?) that I have tweaked a little so as to put it into better, more logically compelling quasi-scientific terms. So, I suppose to be absolutely accurate, when I claim to be presenting six new arguments against the existence of God, I am presenting two absolutely new and original arguments and four arguments I have transformed to a greater or lesser degree. These include two arguments that I have transformed so radically and developed along such markedly different lines as to be virtually unrecognisable from the original arguments along those lines. In the other two arguments (which are actually weaker arguments concerning why people should not believe in God rather than absolute disproofs of God's existence) I have transformed the expression and presentation more than the substance of the original arguments. This is not bad as very few people have found any original arguments concerning the existence of God in the philosophy of religion – St. Anselm found one, George Berkeley found one and Immanuel Kant found one. So I do not consider it bad to have found two completely original arguments and two radical reformulations of arguments, especially as I contend my arguments are valid whereas those of Anselm, Berkeley, Kant and others are not valid.

Another point I should make at the outset is that the six arguments for atheism I am putting are all strictly logical arguments and have been deliberately designed to be completely logical arguments. Therefore I have expressed them in very logical form. Although the logic is rather simple and I have made some effort to keep the language relatively simple, the result is that this may not always make for easy or exciting reading. However I hope readers will make every effort to understand what I am saying because what I am attempting is significant. This is perhaps the first production in a book of a coherent series of logical disproofs of the existence of God as well as closely argued and completely logical reasons why people should not believe in the existence of God. Many philosophers (including many of those generally considered to be the greatest philosophers, such as Descartes, Leibniz and Kant) attempted, albeit unsuccessfully (at least according to most modern opinions) to prove logically the existence of God. Yet no significant philosopher has ever attempted logical disproofs of God's existence. Indeed only a few people in history (such as Carneades and the Indian Carvakas) have ventured, let alone written, anything in the direction of disproving God's existence. Considering that religions, especially monotheistic religions have been so important in the affairs of the world right up to the present day, I think that my efforts are important. I aim to demonstrate first that any belief in God is illogical and second that God's existence can be logically disproved (indeed disproved by relatively simple logical disproofs). That is very important. I therefore hope that readers will put up with some ugliness in the format and presentation of this book. Please understand that my main concern is to establish and demonstrate the strict and complete logicality of all my arguments for atheism.

As I point out elsewhere (The Universal Uncertainty Argument – Prologue) the attempt to logically prove or disprove the existence of God has now become unfashionable to say the least. However up until the nineteenth century it was fashionable (and almost expected) for the most prominent philosophers (such as Descartes, Locke, Leibniz etc) to attempt to prove the existence of God by logical means. In fact in calling this book The Six Ways Of Atheism, I am rather throwing down the gauntlet at the most famous and orthodox attempt, that of St. Thomas Aquinas (1224/5-1274), to prove the existence of God which is traditionally called The Five Ways. All of Aquinas' arguments (which incidentally were not original to him but derived mainly from the ancient Greeks and were merely collected and formalised by him) are now considered invalid, at least by most people. Perhaps that is an indication I should have resisted this title. However as there is no such corpus of formally recognised arguments for atheism, I thought the title of this book somewhat appropriate though I am sure my arguments are, unlike Aquinas', logically valid.

There are some prominent arguments for atheism that I am not including in my Six Ways Of Atheism. The reason is that such arguments, primarily the arguments concerning scientific disproof of God and the human psychology arguments are not valid arguments against the existence of God. Nor so far as I can see can they be adjusted to make them into valid arguments. The Science Disproves God's Existence line of argument became popular and influential when Charles Darwin (1809-1882) showed that the biblical account of Creation in Genesis is scientifically wrong. Other scientists also proved that the world is not six thousand years old but many millions of years old. The problem with such arguments is that while they rightly discredited religions and disproved the truth of religious scriptures, they did not disprove the existence of a monotheistic God as such. Naturally most theologians were then relatively quick to downgrade their scriptures such as The Bible into the status of allegory rather than the God-given literal truth those same scriptures had previously been supposed to be! So Science and scientific advances became ultimately more of an argument against religious scriptures and myths than against a monotheistic God! The fallacy in using Science as an argument against God is that the spheres which Science and Religion deal with (or at least should deal with) are rather different. Most sciences (such as Biology, Chemistry and Geology) describe or theorise with evidence about the world as it is rather than philosophise about questions such as our ultimate creation, mastery of the Universe and good and evil which are more properly the themes of philosophy and possibly religion. Of course in the past, but less so now, religious faiths, particularly in their scriptures, did stray into what is now the domain of Science. They have with recent (in the last few centuries) discoveries been beaten back by scientific disproofs of some of their doctrines and they suffered a consequent loss of credibility and therefore faith in religion. However nowadays most religions have become more circumspect about straying into scientifically resolvable questions and have generally (except for the unworldly 'fundamentalists') downgraded their previous attempts in that direction into allegory and myth. It should be said that in the other direction some sciences such as Physics and Astronomy (at the extremes of those subjects) have also developed a tendency to stray into realms that cannot be properly supported, let alone examined or tested by genuine scientific evidence and observations (even without ever supposing that Science can prove or disprove the existence of God as an ultimate creator or an omnipotent and omniscient being lurking behind or within the whole Universe). I mean here that scientists are unable for example to detect how many asteroids there are between the planets Mars and Jupiter or what planets of the Sun exist beyond Pluto within our own solar system. Yet those same scientists are wont to talk about the very edges of the Universe and the exact happenings within a second or two of the supposed Big Bang! So notwithstanding historic incursions of religions into the scientific domain and incursions of scientists into highly speculative areas that are way beyond the evidence for, let alone the testability, of their theses, Science of itself cannot disprove monotheism because the concept of monotheism is seemingly beyond the reach of Science. However I contend that monotheism is not beyond the reach of even elementary logic which is an entirely different matter. Indeed I say everything that exists must exist within the parameters of Logic and there can be no existence or at least no reliable and no predictable existence outside or beyond the realms of rationality.

The other popular (and mainly nineteenth century) lines of arguments for atheism which I have neglected because I believe they are invalid are the psychological arguments against the existence of God. Although the ancient Athenian leader Critias (c460-403BC) claimed that rulers cunningly invented Gods for their own purposes to keep their populace under control, psychological arguments were popularised by Ludwig Feuerbach (1804-1872) in *The Essence Of Christianity*. Feuerbach argued that the concept of God is merely a psychological invention of the human mind and is therefore false. Karl Marx and Sigmund Freud followed up with similar arguments that God is only a convenient invention of the human mind for the psychological use of mankind. The essential fallacy in such psychological arguments that cannot be remedied is that even if God arose so far as humans are concerned only as a useful psychological notion embedded in the human mind, nevertheless God may then also exist outside of the human mind as well as within the human mind. What the human mind thinks, and the usefulness of the concept of God to humanity, neither proves nor disproves that God also actually exists independently outside and beyond the human mind! For instance, by way of analogy, Europeans before the time of Christopher Columbus may or may not have believed that other as yet undiscovered continents existed in the world (indeed some of them did believe this while many disbelieved it). However the beliefs of ancient Europeans as to the existence or non-existence of undiscovered continents was not even evidence, let alone proof, as to whether other continents existed or not! Similarly the psychological beliefs of humans (or even the usefulness or otherwise of such beliefs) as to whether God exists or not is not even evidence, let alone proof, as to whether God actually exists or not beyond the human mind. Human psychology is just not proof of the realities and unrealities beyond the human mind. I can see no way in which the various psychological arguments against the existence of God can overcome this fundamental fallacy inherent within them!

Another matter I do not aim to deal with and do not wish to cover in this book are the many and various arguments for the existence of God. I suppose I could logically state that if my arguments against the existence of God are valid there cannot be any valid proof of the existence of God. However in any event the general consensus of opinion is that none of these arguments, at least in their present and usual formulations are valid or decisive as arguments for the existence of God. If anybody should be interested in refutations of the most popular arguments for the existence of God these are provided briefly by Bertrand Russell in *Why I Am Not A Christian*. Immanuel Kant in *A Critique Of Pure Reason* refuted more fully the main intellectual arguments for the existence of God (except his own).

A further matter I do not wish to deal with is the question of the usefulness or otherwise to mankind of belief in the existence of God. The questions of whether belief in God has been or indeed still is useful or not to mankind is essentially an entirely different question to the question whether God actually in fact exists. The question of whether belief in God, even if it is a mythical belief, has been or is useful to mankind is really a sociological and psychological question rather than a logical question. No doubt much can be said on both sides of that question but it is no part of the aim of this book to engage in that historical discussion. I use the term 'historical discussion' because the logical proof of the non-existence of God will in future doubtless affect the sustainability of belief in God irrespective of whether such belief is useful or not. It is of course one thing for people to believe as a matter of faith in an entity that may or may not exist but it is rather another thing for people to believe in an entity that has been logically proved not to exist.

Nor do I really wish to deal with my own personal status. Essentially the arguments I put are valid or invalid irrespective of who puts them and irrespective of whether they are original to me or not. It is the arguments that I want to be considered, not the person putting the arguments. Unfortunately in philosophy there is something of an intellectual snobbery around that implies an argument can only be considered seriously if it is put by an academic or at the very least somebody preeminent in some other field. Of course an argument as such is neither enhanced nor diminished by the status of the person putting it but the world is inclined to forget that, particularly in philosophy. For instance nobody would even bat an eyelid if somebody became a multi-millionaire in business without ever having been to business school. Yet professionals in philosophy and religion are wont unlike business studies teachers (who manifestly have no option) to believe that only they or their fellow professionals can now succeed in their chosen subject. You may ask why I should succeed in disproving the existence of God when either valid proof or disproof of the existence of God has eluded millions upon millions of people in the past? Who am I to answer that question except to the extent of pointing out that I have approached the matter in rather novel ways? So I won't discuss either my circumstances or myself personally. Let the arguments I am introducing just speak for themselves and stand or fall on their own inherent merits as arguments!

It is essential in these arguments to understand at least in outline what the concept of a monotheistic God actually entails. God in monotheism is not just a word but is necessarily a concept that entails some absolute qualities (and in this it differs very substantially, indeed radically, from the concepts of God in polytheism).

So we should begin with an examination of the concept of a monotheistic God. I acknowledge that it may be thought presumptuous to even talk in terms of an analysis of God. So it may be more appropriate to think of God in terms of the <u>essential defining qualities of God.</u> Through such essential defining qualities (or characteristics) we should be able to understand the basic meaning of the concept of God, if not the nuances nor the workings of a potential God.

Until perhaps about 1930 there was a consensus, both popular and academic over what was meaned by the term God. Now there is no longer such an academic consensus over the meaning of God but there certainly is still a reasonable popular consensus over the meaning of the term God.

René Descartes (1596-1650), known as the Father of modern philosophy, wrote 'I conceive a God who is sovereign, eternal, infinite, unchangeable, all-knowing, all-powerful and universal Creator of all things outside himself' (Third Meditation). The idea that God can be defined or conceived by his qualities precedes Descartes. It is found in Sextus Empiricus (c200AD) and via 'the negative way' (i.e. God is not mortal, not limited in power etc) in Dionysius The Areopagite (c500AD) and Maimonides (1135-1204). I myself would assert that God's qualities, God's essential defining qualities, are that he must be 'eternal, omnipotent, omniscient, omnipresent, consciously controlling, supremely good, our ultimate creator and our purpose giver.' I differ somewhat (as do others) from Descartes in adding the dimensions of supreme goodness and endowing purpose to the Universe and more tentatively that of omnipresence. However the real point is that there are certain qualities such as immortality which an entity must have in order to be a monotheistic God. For instance if an entity is mortal, if he might die tomorrow or indeed might already have died, that entity cannot be God. How can a dead entity, or an entity in danger of dying possibly be a sensible object of religion? The absence of certain other qualities would also mean that it is absurd to think of an entity deficient in that way as God. How can an entity be God if it is not omnipotent at least to the extent that no entity can be more powerful than it? How can an entity be God if it is not omniscient and so is not fully aware of all that is going on in the Universe, and so unaware for instance of whether there might be some greater entity lurking somewhere unbeknown to it in the Universe? How can an entity be God in the sense that it is worthy of religious awe and worship if it is not supremely good or if indeed some entity within the Universe may be morally better than it is?

Of course if one refers to The Bible the qualities of immortality, creator, omnipotence, omniscience and supreme goodness are attached to the monotheistic God. These essential godly qualities (omnipotence, omniscience, immortality etc) are concordant with the traditions and Scriptures of monotheism, and thus are attached to God in the popular imagination. They are also intellectually essential to God because no entity can possibly exist as a monotheistic God in an intellectual sense in the absence of such qualities. We may not be able to understand how God is omniscient, that is the mechanics of God's omniscience, but we can be sure that God must be omniscient if he is really to be God. In the absence of omniscience he and we could not be confident of his status as God (because in his ignorance there may then exist something more knowledgeable or more powerful than he is). Likewise with immortality. We may not be able to understand how God is immortal but we can be sure that God must be immortal because a dead god either in the future or now is no God. Likewise with God's supreme goodness and his other qualities. So we can be confident at least of knowing what some of God's essential defining qualities must be.

There has of course generally been some tradition of seeing God as being mysterious and beyond human comprehension. However if somebody believes both that God cannot be comprehended by humans and also that God does exist, it must be asked how can one possibly know that God actually exists if one cannot comprehend God? There is an illogicality, a comprehension paradox here – 'God is beyond human comprehension: I comprehend that God exists.' So it is paradoxical and thus untenable to shelter behind God's alleged mysteriousness or our ignorance in promoting a doctrine of knowledge of God's existence. Of course it can still be mysterious how God might achieve omnipotence, omniscience and creation. However to assert one's knowledge that God exists one must also be able to know that God does achieve omnipotence, omniscience, creation and several other things as well.

Relatively recently some academics have attempted to break completely with a definition of God in terms of his defining qualities and have come up with other ways of defining God. Paul Tillich (1886-1965) thought of God merely as our 'ultimate concern'. Later one of his followers, Bishop John Robinson in his famous book Honest To God (published in 1963) described God more simply as 'ultimate reality'. I rather suspect this was mere subterfuge to define God into existence. Bishop Robinson wrote, 'God is, by definition, ultimate reality. And one cannot argue whether ultimate reality exists. One can only ask what ultimate reality is like.' Admittedly a few unconventional theists had attempted redefinitions of God to suit themselves in past ages. Spinoza (1632-1677) had practically redefined God as 'Nature' but he was really a pantheist rather than a monotheist and Swedenborg (1688-1772) had suggested that 'God is Love'. However it has only been in the twentieth century in the wake of the fashion for seeing philosophy primarily in linguistic terms that redefining the term God has become common and almost orthodox in academic circles.

Yet the modernist notion that God is just 'ultimate reality' or our 'ultimate concern' is contrary to Scriptural and traditional monotheism which gives God a personal identity. Ultimate concern or ultimate reality is of course not necessarily religious. There must also be a question whether reality can indeed be legitimately divided into 'ultimate' and other types of reality. There is also the problem that reality and I suppose ultimate reality encompasses much evil which is incompatible with a worthwhile worshipful religious notion of God. Perhaps 'ultimate reality' may ultimately even be meaningless. Furthermore we humans certainly cannot know the full scope of reality as we see such a small sample of it. So we humans cannot possibly be in a legitimate position to assert that ultimate reality is equivalent to God. However from what little we may possibly see of ultimate reality it is a neutral concept whereas God is an extremely positive concept entailing supreme goodness, positive control, omniscience and consciousness (whereas reality as such may not be conscious). Finally, the proposed redefinitions of God, though they may seem just to be neat linguistic tricks, really entail a fundamental logical fallacy. Although it is questionable whether the presumption that a separate ultimate reality really exists is true, the big logical fallacy is to assume without supporting proof or even supporting evidence that 'ultimate reality' (or 'ultimate concern') is God. Of course once it is postulated and assumed that 'ultimate reality' is God, God might perhaps be shown to exist but it is wrong to assume in the first place that 'ultimate reality' is God.

So we are left with the original definition or defining qualities of God. God then is to be properly understood as an entity or phenomenon that must be eternal, omnipotent, omniscient, omnipresent, consciously controlling, supremely good, our ultimate creator and our purpose giver. This is because the God of a monotheistic religion cannot not be eternal, omniscient, consciously controlling, supremely good, our ultimate creator and our purpose giver (and if such qualities are to exist at all God also cannot not be omnipotent and omnipresent) – otherwise he would not be God. In polytheistic religions Gods, at least the main Gods, normally have the quality of being 'eternal'. They are immortal, at least into all the future, if not necessarily all the way back into the past. They also hold if not absolute 'omnipotence' and 'conscious control', at least the power to control and presumably omnipotence over a certain sector of the Universe, be it the sea or death or destruction or whatever they are gods of. So though there is not as much to go on in polytheism as in monotheism by way of absolute, defining qualities, there is still usually something to consider, identify and work on. To return now to monotheism, whatever else may be mysterious about a monotheistic God we can at least identify what are some of God's defining qualities, assuming God exists.

So on this basis we can now go on to the next steps in our investigation of the question whether people should believe in the existence of God or not.

First, I will mention the two arguments I am going to present which are not absolute disproofs of the existence of God but are overwhelming arguments why humans should not believe in the existence of God.

The first such argument is the Man And God Comprehension Gulf Argument. The essential argument there (which is elaborated in the chapter concerning this argument) is that we being humans and limited in scope (for instance being mortal, not immortal) are unable to identify God. For instance we humans may be unable to distinguish between a very long lived entity and an immortal entity. We humans are unable to distinguish between a great power, a daemon and a genuine God even if God did exist. Indeed with our human limitations we humans can have no valid method of identifying God. So we humans could not logically possibly be sure of identifying even a genuine God. And as powerful daemons are likely to be more numerous than God (who by the very definition of monotheism there can only be either one or none of) we would be foolish to believe in anything as God.

The second argument I present why we humans should not actually believe in the existence of a monotheistic God is the God Has No Explanatory Value Argument. Here one should begin with the assumption that even if it might not be logically impossible that God exists, in the absence of valid positive evidence for God's existence it is contrary to proper scientific and intellectual standards to believe in the existence of God. Furthermore positing the existence of God actually ultimately explains nothing and so has no real explanatory value. Everything that God supposedly explains such as the creation of our Universe leaves a yet bigger question of how an even more remarkable entity, namely God, than that which is to be explained can possibly itself be explained. So in terms of explanations, God far from merely having no explanatory value is actually an unwarranted complication and enhancement of the mystery to be explained.

These two arguments are valid ways of showing that we should not believe in the existence of God even if they fail to absolutely disprove the possible existence of God. Yet better still would be to find arguments that can actually disprove the existence of God (rather than merely showing why humans should not believe in God). Unfortunately until now people generally seem not to have put their minds to looking for possible methods or techniques for disproving the existence of God. Although it is not too difficult an intellectual task I can lay claim to originality here. I can myself think of four theoretical circumstances in which God's existence can legitimately be said to be disproved. They are:

1. If God's existence is shown to be so very improbable that there can only be an infinitesimal chance, which is in practical effect no chance, that God actually exists.

2. If God's existence is found to be wholly incompatible with certain aspects of the world, which is after all in conventional religious thought God's creation.

3. If any of God's essential characteristics are mutually incompatible.

4. If any of God's essential characteristics cannot possibly exist.

The first method of disproving God's existence might be somewhat controversial but at any rate it would if substantiated at least prove that nobody can sensibly believe in God. The other three methods of disproof are logically irrefutable as techniques: all they need is successful application in arguments against the existence of God.

I will deal first with arguments against the existence of God which attempt to render God's existence so highly improbable as to be of infinitesimal likelihood in theory and therefore no likelihood in practice. Let us look at some such arguments.

There is what I call the God Is Many Sided Argument. This is a traditional argument against belief in God. It points out that practically everybody who believes in God has a rather different notion of God to everybody else. Therefore the notion of God practically every individual person believes in must according to this argument and logically be erroneous and not reflect an existent God. The situation is as David Hume (1711-1776) described it in his Natural History Of Religion, 'scarce any two men have ever agreed precisely in the same (religious) sentiments'. So any individual's personal vision of God is unlikely to be correct because it is substantially different from practically every other individual's version of God. Even within each religion, Christianity, Judaism and Islam there are sects and within each sect there are individual interpretations that differ substantially from each other, even among priests. Though ecumenism has been in fashion in the twentieth century, there is inescapably a fundamental difference at least for us as to whether on pain of Hell one must follow Christ and the Trinitarian personal God or the impersonal Allah who exists only in one form. The real point of this argument is that because of the many millions of different versions of God there is only an infinitesimal chance that any particular version is correct. To the nearest percentage point that is equivalent to saying there is zero chance that a particular belief in God is correct. So we may effectively say our version (or indeed any particular version) of God does not exist and so for us God does not exist.

Then there is what I call the Time And Space Argument against the existence of God. This argument is also a traditional argument and is somewhat similar to the last argument. The argument here is that belief in God is primarily a matter of sociological circumstances whereas the God Is Many Sided Argument concentrated more particularly on the idiosyncratic element of belief in God. Anyhow the Time And Space Argument starts from the premise that different people in different societies and at different times have believed in very many different Gods. Therefore at least most, if not all, the Gods people have believed in cannot exist. Therefore it is statistically practically impossible that the God any particular theist now believes in actually exists. Put more bluntly the argument is that people have usually held their religious beliefs in accordance with the age and society they have lived in. Therefore most religious belief (be it Christian, Moslem, Hindu, Buddhist or some variety of pagan) has evidently everything to do with the culture and society people live in and nothing to do with God. Furthermore as religions contradict each other in many fundamentals either the great majority of people or all people have been wrong in holding their religious beliefs. So surely it is too great a coincidence for any one person to expect he has the good fortune to be born into the society which has (or even for himself to adopt) the correct religious belief if such there be. Indeed all or all except one religious beliefs must be mistaken. And judging by the laws of averages – which must apply – even if atheism were not the correct view it is highly unlikely that any adopted religion among the many religions that exist and the many more that have existed is correct. So as the overwhelming number of religious beliefs are patently and necessarily wrong, as are most or all versions of God, it is reasonable and sensible to hold that for all practical purposes all the proffered versions of some God existing are wrong.

So far one might respond by suggesting that all these two traditional arguments have shown to be of infinitesimal likelihood is that any particular religious version of God is correct, not that God itself in whatsoever form probably does not exist. Whether the concept of God can be so readily divorced from all religious forms of God or indeed whether the concept of God is of much value if divorced from all religion and all religious description is debatable. However the argument I develop in this book, The Aggregate Of Qualities Argument, goes further. It renders not merely our religious versions of God but also the very concept of a monotheistic God itself so improbable, so infinitesimally probable, that one might fairly say God does not exist. Let me summarise that argument.

Belief in God involves not one, but several improbable steps. 'God' is a blanket term entailing many things. A precondition for God existing is the inherently unlikely proposition that one (there can only be one, if any) omnipotent (or at any rate 'maximally powerful') entity exists. So we start with a very unlikely assumption. But how much more unlikely is it that if one omnipotent entity does exist, it is the best in terms of goodness (a very different quality to sheer power!) of all the millions of millions of entities that exist? Even that is an understatement – it is supposedly the only entity to have attained absolute goodness. Not only is it absolutely good and omnipotent but it also happens to uniquely be the conscious controller and creator of the Universe and be eternal and much more besides! How improbable is an entity that has all these qualities? Even ignoring the evidence for the non-existence of at least some of the necessary godly qualities, the improbability of the chance combination of all these qualities in one entity (out of countless millions of possible entities) is weighty circumstantial evidence for atheism. Indeed because there is at most only one omnipotent entity among a practically infinite number of entities, there is only an infinitesimal chance, effectively no chance, that the one possible omnipotent entity is also the most morally good entity in the Universe (particularly since power and moral goodness are completely separate qualities!). So there is on this aggregate of qualities argument only an infinitesimal, effectively no, chance of God existing.

The various probabilistic arguments argue not that it is absolutely impossible that God exists but that there is so infinitesimally small a chance that God exists that God's possible existence can and should be discounted by us. This line of argument that God's existence is really so improbable that the possibility should be discounted does validly show the conceptual difficulties entailed in theistic belief that lurk behind the one conglomerate word 'God'.

Incidentally this general line of argumentation deriving from improbability is (unlike other arguments in this book, excepting those concerned with human identification or self-identification of any God) as applicable to polytheistic Gods as to a monotheistic God. This is because polytheistic religions (such as Hinduism) do not usually make the mistake of endowing their Gods with as many absolute qualities as monotheism does, qualities which in the end can turn out to be impossible qualities. Indeed polytheistic Gods cannot have many absolute qualities because as there are many 'gods' in polytheism most of them cannot be omnipotent or our creator etc. This leaves such polytheistic religions and polytheistic Gods vulnerable mainly (though not exclusively, as their Gods also have the identification and even self-identification problems that monotheistic Gods have) to the charge that there are so many differing and indeed conflicting versions of polytheism that it is impossible that most of them can be true. There is seemingly only an infinitesimal likelihood that any of the many versions of polytheism around both now and in the past is in fact correct. Therefore statistically speaking one can legitimately claim that there is no real likelihood of any particular version of polytheism being correct. This unlikelihood is so great to all practical intents and purposes as to count as an actual statistical disproof of any particular version of polytheism being true.

The second method of argument (that the known world is actually incompatible with the existence of God) is by far the most common method of argument that has been used in the past against the existence of God. The orthodox form of this argument is the argument against the existence of God deriving from suffering and evil in the world. The usual argument is that the world is incompatible with the existence of God because if God exists he is necessarily supremely good and supremely powerful and created our world but there are elements in the world such as evil and suffering which are incompatible with its creation by a good God. This line of argument is logically correct. As God is sovereign over the whole Universe if any part of the Universe including our world is incompatible with God's existence then God cannot exist (after all we know the Universe actually exists but are not sure that God exists). Indeed nobody even really attempts to dispute that logic. However what is disputed by theists is that our world, indeed even the apparently worst or evil features of our world, is in reality evil in an overall sense and thus incompatible with the existence of God. As it conventionally stands the discussions over such things as the primacy of freewill or the necessity of some apparent evil to highlight the good are indeed complex but I think there is scope for strengthening the atheistic argument. This is what I aim to achieve in The This Is Not The Best Possible World Argument featured in this book. In that argument I contend that if God exists God must be not merely good but supremely good and our supremely powerful creator. Then it follows logically that the world must not merely be good in an overall sense but must be the best possible world, and not the best possible world in just some parts but the best possible world right through. Therefore the argument should be not merely that God is incompatible with a bad world, but God is incompatible with anything at all that falls short of being the best possible world. Furthermore it is possible to show – what common sense tells us anyhow – that we do not live in the best possible world. The method of doing this is to show that in many vital matters there is no consistency in the world. So even though we humans may not be able to absolutely know what is actually the best possible thing, we can know that contradictory things such as some people being born sighted, some being born partially sighted and some being born blind cannot all constitute the best possible state of things. However if this is not the best possible world in every way that omnipotence and supreme goodness can create, God who must by definition be both omnipotent and supremely good cannot exist. So this argument that this is not the best possible world is a disproof of the existence of God.

The third possible method of rational atheistic argument is to argue that some of God's essential characteristics are mutually incompatible with each other. If this were proved God could not exist. The usual characteristic of God to be seen as incompatible with his other characteristics is his 'immutability' because of course immutability would stifle change and so stifle divine action. However I am not myself convinced that 'immutability' need in fact be an essential characteristic of God. Obviously God's own essential characteristics such as his immortality, omnipotence, omniscience and supreme goodness cannot be changed but I rather think that the pattern within the Universe can be changed just as a pattern within a kaleidoscope can be changed. Indeed I would personally go further and suggest that a varying, dynamic, mutable pattern within the Universe might be preferable to a static, immutable Universe. So I conclude that no necessary incompatibility exists between say God's role as creator of our world and God's other qualities. God need not be immutable except in his own essential characteristics and even in his supreme goodness he can make changes in the Universe provided all parts of the Universe are at all times as good as they can realistically be. So questions such as if the world is so perfect now why did not God create it earlier, do not necessarily arise. Therefore this line of argumentation that God's essential qualities conflict with each other, though worthy of further investigation and valid as an approach, is as I see it not validated in practice and so is not logically proved. So at present this method of argument is contributing nothing to the disproof of God's existence because no valid disproof of God's existence along these lines has yet been found.

The fourth and final method of argument I can think of that can be used for actually disproving the existence of God is proving some or any of God's essential characteristics inherently cannot logically exist. I have already in this Introduction in analysing what the concept of a monotheistic God necessarily entails listed eight essential qualities a monotheistic God must have. God must be eternal, omnipotent, omniscient, omnipresent, consciously controlling, supremely good, our ultimate creator and our purpose giver. An investigation is therefore needed to see which if any of these essential qualities that a monotheistic God must have inherently cannot exist or at any rate cannot coexist with the Universe as it is. I have carried out this investigation in my chapter on Some Of God's Defining Qualities Cannot Exist Argument. To summarise the results of that investigation, I cannot find any proof that three of the necessary qualities (i.e. being eternal, consciously controlling and our ultimate creator) cannot exist at least hypothetically. The situation with three of the other essential qualities, omnipresence, supreme goodness and omnipotence, is I think somewhat unclear and debatable. Indeed omnipotence is the one quality of God which has historically been debated along these lines. That debate has reached something of a draw with both sides yielding some ground. Theists have generally yielded that absolute omnipotence is impossible while non-theists have generally accepted that 'maximal power' is sufficient for God. In respect of omniscience I argue in detail (The Universal Uncertainty Argument) that that quality is inherently impossible primarily because there is no possible means of being certain of one's own omniscience especially regarding the future. Therefore nothing, not even a potential God, could possibly be certain of its own omniscience. Therefore as the quality of omniscience is logically inherently unattainable, no thing, not even a potential God can be omniscient even though omniscience is an essential quality for God. So one must conclude as a matter of logic that neither an omniscient being nor God can possibly exist. However in this book I concentrate my argument in Some Of God's Defining Qualities Cannot Exist on the essential quality in a monotheistic God of being our purpose giver. In summary I argue that it is essential that a monotheistic God gives us a significant ultimate purpose. Furthermore we humans must be aware of that purpose so as to underpin morality and to make the purpose (which God as a supremely good and powerful entity must give to the world) meaningful to us. However I also argue that there neither is nor can be ultimate purpose in the world. Therefore a potential God not only does not but also cannot supply ultimate purpose to our world. Therefore it is impossible even though it is necessary for a potential God to genuinely be our purpose giver. So I conclude it is definitively thereby logically proved that a monotheistic God cannot and therefore does not actually exist.

So there it is – six atheistic proofs are presented to readers in this book. Some of these proofs are logically absolutely conclusive in proving not merely that God should not be believed in but also that God cannot possibly actually exist.

Of course in this Introduction I have only summarised these six arguments. Indeed I have summarised these six arguments within the context of a wider picture of the philosophy of religion, particularly in respect of the general techniques I am advocating as valid techniques for disproving the existence of God. It is in the individual chapters (one devoted to each argument) that I set out these six substantially innovative arguments in fuller detail and in which I try to foresee and respond to possible objections that may be made to each argument. So please read on and look into these arguments in more detail with me.

CHAPTER 1

The Aggregate of Qualities Argument

A. Prologue

This is an argument concerning the likelihood or unlikelihood of any single entity possessing all the various qualities God must have if he is to be God. The argument involves first analysing God's main qualities. Then it considers whether each of these qualities is rare or even unique, assuming they are even capable of existing in some entity. It then considers the statistical chance of all those qualities existing in combination in only one entity – that is in what would be God. This assessment in statistical terms of the chances of a combinative effect of the essential monotheistic qualities into only one entity is the main insight of this argument. Finally it argues that if there is only the most infinitesimal chance of such qualities existing in combination that is in practical effect and in statistical terms the equivalent of showing there is effectively no chance of these qualities existing in combination in one entity. Therefore in statistical terms there is effectively the equivalent to no chance of God existing.

This argument is so far as I know original. Yet in its probabilistic nature it is rather similar to less abstract arguments one can put and indeed people from time to time have put about whether any particular version of monotheism is correct. As David Hume (1711-1776), a Scottish philosopher wrote (in his Introduction to his Natural History Of Religion) in the context of religion, 'scarce any two men have ever agreed precisely in the same sentiments'. Thus one may argue that even if God did exist it is highly unlikely that it is the Christian version of God that exists. After all even among monotheists there are presently Jewish, Islamic, Sikh and other versions of God. Of course in human historical terms other versions of God have also been worshipped in the past. Indeed this is only among humans, let alone among other possible entities in the Universe. So in probabilistic terms it is highly unlikely to say the least that even if God exists, it is the Christian version of God that exists. Then even if one were to suppose, unlikely though it is, that it is a Christian version of God that exists, there are many conflicting versions of the Christian God that could exist. There are the Roman Catholic, Lutheran, Anglican, Eastern Orthodox, Maronite, Coptic and Methodist versions of God (all somewhat different from each other) to name but a few. So even if God were by some remote chance or fluke to be a Christian version of God, one still has a very small chance indeed of believing in the version of Christianity (if any such exists) among the very many versions of Christianity that actually accords with God. Furthermore most versions or sects of Christianity be it Anglican, Catholic or whatever tend to have both a traditionalist conservative wing and a liberal wing. Indeed to complicate matters even further these wings tend to exist on each of many different issues, be it liturgy, abortion, doctrine or whatever. Furthermore some of those who see God as supporting traditionalism on some issues may well believe that God favours a liberal approach on other issues! Indeed the very vision and doctrine of God proclaimed by even any two priests is seldom quite the same. So the net result is that there are endless millions of versions, conflicting versions of God that have been put forward. Therefore this analysis shows (to develop this argument into my terms) there is only an infinitesimal chance even if God exists, indeed even given the remote possibility that the Christian God exists, any particular person is believing in quite the correct version of God and religion! This clearly valid argument concerning belief in relation to statistical chance shows there is only the most infinitesimal chance that any particular person believes in the correct version of religion or even the kind of God that actually exists, even if any God were to exist. I therefore say that given the millions upon millions of differing versions of God, there is in effect no chance that any particular person, including oneself (and including all priests) believes in the correct version of religion and in an accurate version of God!

So there are so many possible versions of religion that by the sheer laws of chance nobody can have any sensible hope of believing in the correct type of religion and the correct version of God even if God were to exist. Such is – and should be – the power of numbers and arithmetic to produce a valid argument. The sheer logic of statistics properly applied can indeed amount to an overwhelming and valid argument that throws light upon what may otherwise be a very confused situation. In essence the aggregate of qualities argument works to throw light on the likelihood or otherwise of God existing by using an arithmetical, statistical analysis of the topic.

So we are going to apply this principle of evaluating things statistically to the question of God's very existence. Let us therefore turn from the conceptually simpler and more graphic question of whether any particular version of human religion has any realistic statistical chance of being correct to the more abstract question of God's essential qualities.

Belief in God involves not one, but several improbable steps. God is a blanket term entailing many things. A precondition for God to exist is the inherently unlikely proposition that one (there can only be one, if any) omnipotent entity exists. I say that it is very unlikely to start with, but how much more unlikely is it that if one omnipotent entity actually does exist, it is the best in terms of goodness of all the millions upon millions of entities that exist? That is an understatement – it is supposedly the only entity to have attained absolute goodness. Not only is this hypothetical entity absolutely good and omnipotent but it also happens actually to be exercising conscious control over all the Universe. You may think such a creature would die sometime from all its efforts! But no, by chance it is eternal. Not only that, it somehow has – probably unlike anything else (unique again!) – the resources to be omniscient as well. Then it alone of all possible things which could make life meaningful in the unlikely event that it is meaningful makes the whole of life meaningful. Any one of the qualities mentioned above (omnipotence, omniscience, absolute goodness, being consciously controlling, eternal and creating purpose) in any entity would be almost inconceivable and not imply the existence of the other qualities in that same entity. How very improbable (assuming it is even possible to have all or any of these qualities) is an entity that has all these qualities in combination! Even ignoring the evidence for the non-existence of at least some of these qualities, the improbability of the chance combination of all these qualities in one entity (out of countless millions of possible entities) is overwhelming statistical evidence for atheism. Indeed statistically speaking the likelihood of the existence of such an entity as God combining in himself alone all these exceptionally rare, often unique (if even existent) qualities is so infinitesimally small a chance as to be for all practical purposes a zero chance. So the effect of this argument is that in statistical terms there is not even a reasonable chance worth considering that God may exist. Therefore statistically, indeed logically speaking, God does not exist.

B. Summary Of The Argument

1. If God exists, God must necessarily possess all of several remarkable qualities (including supreme goodness, omnipotence, immortality, omniscience, ultimate creator, purpose giver).

2. Every one of these qualities may not exist in any entity and if any such quality does exist it exists in few entities or in some cases (e.g. omnipotence, ultimate creator) in at most one entity.

3. Therefore it is highly unlikely that any entity would possess even one of these qualities.

4. There is an infinitesimal chance that any one entity (given the almost infinite number of entities in the Universe) might possess the combination of even some two of these qualities, let alone all of them.

5. In statistical analysis a merely hypothetical infinitesimal chance can in effect be treated as the no chance to which it approximates so very closely.

6. Therefore as there is statistically such an infinitesimal chance of any entity possessing, as God would have to do, all God's essential qualities in combination it can be said for all practical and statistical purposes that God just does not exist.

C. Explaining The Argument

To appreciate this argument fully one must appreciate that language is great at glossing over reality. If you ask whether a thing exists you are entering into a binary system with two possible answers (akin to a coin falling down Heads or Tails), either that it exists or that it does not exist. There is even a tendency to assume in our minds something near a 50-50 chance of existence or non-existence. Language is not really numerically based, nor are our imaginations and intellects. It is easy to assume for instance the question is there a rabbit in the field is similar to the question is there a white rabbit in the field or the question is there a blue rabbit in the field. The questions though apparently similar in that they all concern a field, rabbits and existence are all very different in actual substance. Asking whether there is a rabbit in a field is probably an open question with a reasonable likelihood that the answer might be yes or no. Asking whether there is a white rabbit in a field is transforming the probabilities heavily (given the actual rarity of white rabbits) into the answer being no although there is some possibility of a positive answer. Asking whether there is a blue rabbit in the field is, since we have no experience of blue rabbits, transforming the question into one that isn't even sensibly worth asking because there is only an infinitesimal chance that there is a blue rabbit in a field. After all it can first properly be asked does a blue rabbit actually exist anywhere and then even if any blue rabbit does exist, how remote a chance is it that a blue rabbit is actually on that field of all possible fields? Thus the binary language of existence or non-existence in each question (as indeed our own mental apparatus also tends to) glosses over the huge degree to which the different questions are weighted in probabilistic terms. However this aggregate of qualities statistically based argument invites us to think in terms of numerical degrees of probability of existence instead of in the conventional merely binary (exist-not exist) language of existence.

The next step in this argument after converting thinking in binary language into thinking in terms of numerical probability is to analyse the proposition being put forward. For instance a white rabbit puts forward the notions of white and rabbit in combination with the phenomenon. It is then therefore not just white nor rabbit but the combination of white and rabbit in the same phenomenon that is being considered. Similarly the concept of God necessarily puts forward the combined notions of omnipotence, absolute goodness, conscious control, immortality, omnipotence, omnipresence, our ultimate creator and creation of purpose to make up, at least in part, the phenomenon of God. It is this combination of at least eight distinctive qualities whose existence or non-existence is being asserted as the term God. God is a word which is in fact a term denoting a unique combination of qualities. Furthermore in the absence of probably any (certainly most) of these eight qualities the phenomenon described would be very remarkable but would not be sufficient to amount to God. (This is for reasons already described in the Introduction to this book – as this is essential to several arguments in this book – and not repeated here.) So God if he exists must combine in himself all these eight remarkable characteristics (at least insofar as they can possibly exist at all in any entity).

The next stage after analysing what God's essential necessary qualities would be is to assess the numerical likelihood that these individual qualities exist in any one particular entity. Obviously this cannot be done exactly but only at best very approximately since there are countless millions upon millions of entities. (I assume just for the purposes of this argument that all these essential qualities of a monotheistic God are at least theoretically capable of existing within some creature.) Let's take the first quality – omnipotence. It is obviously a countless millions to one chance against any entity being the single most powerful creature, let alone an omnipotent creature in the Universe. Indeed in the whole Universe there may well be no omnipotent nor even 'maximally powerful' entity at all in which case there is necessarily no God. Or there may conceivably be a single omnipotent entity but there cannot possibly be more than one omnipotent entity because an omnipotent entity must by definition have the power to exert its will over every other entity. (Of course an omnipotent entity wouldn't be able to exercise its will over a second or third omnipotent entity because in that case that second or third so called omnipotent entity would not actually be omnipotent.) So within the whole Universe among the millions of millions of millions of entities that exist there cannot possibly be more than a single omnipotent entity (and there might well, indeed probably, not even be any omnipotent entity). So there is really in effect only an infinitesimal chance that any single particular entity in the Universe is omnipotent. Of course it might be claimed that that is in itself no great argument since people particularly select the one omnipotent entity that might exist in the Universe to worship as God. However this argument is undoubtedly significant when it is estimated what the likelihood is that the single most powerful entity in the Universe is of the countless millions of entities that exist also in moral terms the single best entity in the Universe (which it must be to be God).

Apart from chance there is no reason why the most powerful entity should also be the morally most perfect (indeed absolutely perfect) entity since there is no real inherent relation between 'most powerful' and 'morally best in its nature'. Yet an entity must combine these two inherently unrelated qualities (omnipotence and moral perfection) if it is to be God. What a forlorn hope it would seem that among countless millions of entities for any particular single entity to be the most powerful (indeed omnipotent) single entity – no entity can have more than an infinitesimal chance of being the most powerful single entity! It is another forlorn hope for any particular entity to be the morally best (indeed morally perfect) single entity among countless millions of entities in the Universe – so no entity can have more than an infinitesimal chance of being the morally best entity! For an entity to combine being the most powerful entity in the whole Universe with being the morally best entity in the whole Universe is surely practically impossible since that combines an absolutely infinitesimal chance with an absolutely infinitesimal chance. Yet added to this combination of infinitesimal chances we must further consider the chances that this same entity happens also to be eternal (though perhaps no entity may actually be eternal) and our purpose-giver (also a unique quality, if even an existent quality) and also consciously controlling (another unique quality, if even an existent quality) and omniscient (though perhaps no entity may actually be omniscient) and omnipresent, not to mention it being our actual creator. There is a very good chance that some or all of these remarkable hypotheticated qualities actually belong to no entity, but there must be an inconceivably infinitesimal chance that all these qualities combine in merely one entity, God.

The next stage of this argument is to assess the actual significance of the statistically absolutely infinitesimal chance that all these qualities are combined within one entity. We should ask how do we respond to such a statistically infinitesimal chance? We have in this argument already reached the stage where we can state that there is (assuming God is not precluded on other grounds from existing) only an infinitesimal chance that God does exist. That follows absolutely accurately from this line of argument. However we might legitimately go a little bit further and correctly state that for practical purposes absolutely infinitesimal chances can properly be ignored and rounded down to zero as not being statistically of any significance. (In the same way analogously we humans probably would totally discount the almost infinitesimal chance of being killed by an earthquake here in England tomorrow. That is justifiable but much less justifiable than discounting the thoroughly infinitesimal chance of God existing.) We sometimes ignore up to one half a per cent, a one in two hundred chance, more so a one in two thousand chance and we usually ignore a one in two million chance and certainly a one in a trillion chance, let alone an actually infinitesimal chance. So as we can know by this aggregate of God's qualities argument that there is an absolutely infinitesimal, practically zero chance of God existing, and as with good reason we ignore a statistically insignificant infinitesimal chance, we can properly say that to the nearest significant number there is a zero chance of God existing. So we can show that in normal terms of statistical significance God clearly does not exist. It is therefore clear in realistic terms that God does not exist. Indeed such a statement is better established than most of our knowledge because almost no knowledge is either absolute or based upon one hundred per cent certainty. Therefore in all normal statistical terms this Aggregate Of Qualities Argument constitutes a complete and valid proof that God does not exist.

D. Possible Objections To The Argument

I shall consider the seven types of possible objections I can presently think of to this statistical argument, this Aggregate Of Qualities Argument against the existence of God. I shall deal with these various conceivable objections in the sections numbered (i) to (vii) below.

(i) Need God Necessarily Have All These Qualities?

The first possible objection that can be raised is the question need God really have the various qualities that are attributed to him as a premise in the aggregate of qualities argument against his existence? The answer is yes. If God lacked such qualities, certainly the most essential of these qualities (omnipotence, omniscience, immortality, supreme goodness, conscious control and being our ultimate creator), he simply would not be God.

For a start a potential God even if he had all the other qualities could not exist as God if he was not eternal. God cannot be a here today, dead tomorrow kind of entity. God cannot be an absurd lame duck type of God whose assurances cannot be guaranteed and whose religion that speaks of eternity (let alone merely the future) is based upon a presumption that even he (God) cannot truthfully vouch for. So an entity that may die sometime or indeed may already have died and so cannot truthfully guarantee to enforce its regime for ever is not God. Similarly God must be supremely good or else he would not exist as God even if he had all the other requisite qualities. After all God is supposed to be worthy of voluntary admiration and worship. Surely if just one entity is to be worshipped voluntarily (as God is supposed to be), then it must be the best of all entities in moral terms if it is to be credible and appropriate as the supreme object of worship! Nor could an entity exist as God and not be omnipotent (at least omnipotent to the maximum possible degree of omnipotence) even if he had all the other qualities requisite to God. An entity that could not necessarily accomplish his own wishes nor even be sure of overcoming all other entities could not in reality be God. Likewise an entity could not exist as God unless it was omniscient and could be sure there is not some other more powerful entity lurking somewhere in the Universe in a realm beyond its knowledge. Additionally, if an entity is to be God (the God of religion) it would also necessarily have to be our ultimate creator. It would also actually have to be exerting its control and power (rather than choosing to abdicate itself from the situation). So there is no doubt that God would have to have at least these essential qualities in order to be God. So, being God must necessarily entail an aggregate or combination of remarkable, indeed generally unique (even if existent) qualities. No entity could be God if it did not contain within itself such an aggregation or combination of all these qualities.

(ii) God's Qualities Are Revealed Through Evidence Not Chance?

The possible objection here is that our appreciation of this combination of remarkable qualities in God has nothing whatsoever to do with chance or an accumulation of chances. Rather this combination of remarkable qualities is evidenced by the various strands we can properly detect through reason or observation that combine together and actually exist within God. According to this objection this combination of qualities naturally flows together and can be observed working together within the evidenced notion (or at least idea) of God.

This is what John Locke (1632-1704) tried to argue in Book 4,

Chapter 10 in An Essay Concerning Human Understanding. In essence, according to Locke, this combination of qualities is necessary for the originator of ourselves to have, without which we humans would not exist – and we clearly do exist! Locke argued that no real Being can be produced from nothing – and so from eternity something must have existed, and all Beings must originate from the same Source 'and so this eternal Being must also be the most powerful'. Knowledge must also have arisen from a knowledgeable being (it being impossible that things wholly devoid of knowledge should produce a Knowing Being) – and so 'there is an eternal, most powerful and most knowing Being... and from this Idea duly considered, will easily be deduced all those Attributes, which we ought to ascribe to this eternal Being.'

However Locke's line of argument is clearly fallacious. For a start lesser things can produce greater things just as greater things can produce lesser things. Albert Einstein's parents, though they were lesser intellects, could produce Albert Einstein's intellect, and so on. Indeed if Locke was correct the march of history would be degenerative with a loss in each generation, each generation being intrinsically worse than its producers (its parents). More fundamentally things need not necessarily be caused anyhow. Also, in any event the causes can be very different to the result (such as hydrogen and oxygen, two gases, producing a liquid, water). So an anthropomorphic model of causation such as applies to a Watch and Watchmaker (with a superior watchmaker producing a watch) clearly cannot properly be extrapolated into a general rule of genesis that applies universally beyond the sphere of human intervention.

However leaving aside John Locke, can there be valid evidence available to us for God's qualities existing and all combining within one entity? I should think not. As finite entities we humans cannot know the absolutely infinite. As mortal entities we cannot recognise for certain what is immortal. We humans are not even in a position to identify with certainty supreme goodness, omniscience, omnipotence, our creator and the provider of purpose. All we might be able to do within our limited human perspective is recognise the absence of such qualities within some entities. But spotting instances where such qualities do not exist is very different to being able to identify where or even whether such qualities do exist.

So this objection is not valid. We humans being limited neither have nor even can have any adequate evidence that any entity possesses any of these absolute qualities (omnipotence, omniscience, immortality etc). The real problem here is that we cannot as humans with our human limitations distinguish between greatly superior to us and omnipotent, very long lived and immortal, very knowledgeable and omniscient etc. We cannot even have any adequate evidence that all these qualities naturally or necessarily occur together. Therefore in assessing whether any entity exists as God we humans necessarily fall far short of being able to obtain any reliable evidence to support the notion of God. I shall consider in the next section whether the qualities essential to God have an inherent or logical tendency to combine.

(iii) Mustn't Some Or All Of God's Qualities Necessarily Be Logically Combined?

The possible objection here would be that these qualities (omnipotence, immortality, omniscience, supreme goodness etc) of God if they do exist anywhere must logically necessarily coexist in one entity, God, because at the highest absolute level they are all inherently concomitant. For instance it can be argued how can an omnipotent entity not be omniscient and an omniscient entity not be omnipotent? Surely an omnipotent entity would have the power to be omniscient himself and a truly omniscient entity could make himself omnipotent by virtue of his knowledge of how to do so?

Is this objection answerable? I believe so. For instance it is at least possible to argue that omnipotence and omniscience are or can be quite separate. One may think of an omniscient entity that is too fragile of body or weak of limb or even mentally reluctant to achieve omnipotence for himself. However one may concede a likely coalescence of some of the qualities (such as omnipotence and omniscience) without conceding any inherent coalescence at all between other qualities (such as omnipotence and supreme goodness). It may be that present 'power' qualities ('omnipotence' and 'omniscience') may coalesce but that has nothing whatsoever to do with 'values' qualities (such as 'supreme goodness') which in turn has nothing to do with the 'eternity' quality ('immortality') which belong in different spheres. There is no logical reason why the most powerful entity that exists should also be morally the best entity and there is little reason for supposing that its present omnipotence shall necessarily endure for all eternity. So it would indeed be an absolutely remarkable thing if there was an omnipotent entity and that same entity was also by nature morally the best entity among the millions upon millions of entities that have existed. Yet God would have to be such a remarkable thing. God could not be a worthy God and so could not be God even if it was omnipotent if indeed it was discovered that some entities were or have been morally better than it! So we are still validly able to genuinely pile or compound some infinitesimal chances (for instance of an entity being omnipotent) upon other infinitesimal chances (for instance of an entity being the best entity in moral terms) to make an absolutely infinitesimal statistical chance of the qualities necessarily essential to God being combined within one entity, God.

So even if the aggregate of genuinely separate qualities that God must have to be God is reduced somewhat by some possible tendency to coalesce among some of the qualities, there would remain a sufficient number of inherently unconnected qualities for this statistical argument still to be valid. There would still be an absolutely infinitesimal chance that the one entity (if existent) that possesses one remarkable quality such as omnipotence is also the very entity to possess a combination of all the other remarkable (yet intrinsically unrelated) characteristics that God must have. So in practice this argument that there is only an infinitesimal chance that all God's qualities, even if existent, reside in only one entity rather than being distributed among sundry entities is not significantly less valid as an argument. Therefore this Aggregate Of Qualities Argument is still valid even if the number of distinct qualities in the aggregate of qualities essential to God is found upon examination to be somewhat reduced.

(iv) Is Probabilism Valid Concerning God?

The possible objection here is that since God would be one and unique he would not be subject to any law of averages nor to any probabilistic form of argument. The principle relied on here is quite plain. For instance we might know statistically that average life expectancy in a particular country is seventy years. That would enable us to say that the average age at death for a thousand people there is seventy or very close to seventy. However we would not really be helped in knowing the age at death of any particular individual there – far from being seventy it could be under one or over one hundred or anything in between. So while the laws of averages would surely apply to a thousand random people considered as a whole, the probabilistic approach may well tell us practically nothing about any particular, still less any unique, individual entity (such as God would have to be).

However the matter would be very different if in the example instead of 1,000 people all dying at different ages and only averaging 70, 999 out of 1,000 people were actually to die at the age of 70. Then we could indeed say that it is overwhelmingly likely that any particular individual does die at the age of 70. And if that were not overwhelming enough, it would be ten times as overwhelming if 9,999 people out of 10,000 died at the age of 70. Indeed there comes a point (say when all except one of many millions of people die at the age of 70) when one can say to all intents and purposes as a matter of fact everybody, including every individual, dies at the age of 70. In effect the sheer weight of statistical probability can be so strong that the probability to all intents and purposes converts itself into a fact (the exception being so exceedingly rare that generally and in normal circumstances it cannot reasonably be significantly considered). And so it is in this case concerning God's non-existence. One can legitimately state that the chance the most powerful entity in the Universe is of all the countless millions of entities in the Universe also the most supremely good entity is so absolutely infinitesimal that it can legitimately be discounted as statistically absolutely insignificant. After all even if there is an omnipotent entity, there is necessarily only one omnipotent entity and so it has only one chance out of countless millions of being by nature the morally best entity out of countless millions of entities. So although God would be unique there is such an infinitesimal chance of God existing merely in terms of statistical probabilities arising from his unique characteristics combining in one and the same entity (out of millions of possible entities) that it can accurately and assuredly be stated in terms of mathematics that God just does not exist. The dice of probabilities is just far too heavily loaded against God's possible existence to make the concept of God existing anything other than a very fanciful proposition that can and should properly be discounted.

So although I admit that insofar as an entity, be it God or anything else, is unique it is not subject to statistical probability yet insofar as any entity, including a potential God, is in any respect one among many entities it is indeed subject to statistical probabilities. For instance a hybrid animal or a dog with four heads may be practically unique in its way and so not subject to statistical analyses of such things as its behaviour that may be affected by those respects in which it is unique but it is not unique in relation to its being an animal. So even it would therefore be subject to the statistical certainty among animals that it is mortal and that it was both born and will inevitably die. Similarly with respect to a potential God it would not be possible to predict statistically how from its unique perspective it would for instance view politics in terms of favouring a right wing or a left wing view. However it would be possible to look at it statistically in relation to those things (such as its likelihood of being the best entity in moral terms) in which it is only one entity among countless millions of entities. This is especially so where there is a random distribution of a quality such as power and morality among the many countless millions of entities. It can therefore legitimately be stated that there is in statistical terms only an infinitesimal chance that the same entity is both the most powerful entity and also the morally best entity in the entire Universe! Therefore it is wrong to claim that a potential God is in no respect subject to statistical and probabilistic analysis. Of course one has to be careful in one's use of statistics in relation to the possibility of God existing as indeed one has to be careful in using statistics in any matter. However in this particular instance of dealing with the distribution of power and moral qualities among entities it is wrong to suggest that a statistical approach (correctly applied) is invalid. So this particular objection to this argument is both incorrect in principle and also incorrect in this particular instance.

(v) Rare Events Often Occur?

The objection here is that unlikely events can and do occur, seemingly contrary to the rules of chance.

My response is that this may seem to be the case but when looked at more closely and rationally this is seldom the case and the laws of chance are correct in an overall sense.

In the first place one should distinguish between merely improbable events and extremely improbable events. For instance if one throws a dice it is not likely to result in a three coming up but one in six times it will result in a three coming up – so though a three is a bit unlikely it is not very unlikely and will happen quite frequently. However that is different to winning the jackpot in a national lottery – though somebody will win, it is unlikely to be any particular individual for whom one might predict a win beforehand. The chances of being hit and killed by a meteorite from Mars are even more unlikely, so much so that it will probably not happen to anybody alive today. So unlikely events do occur frequently but extremely unlikely events seldom occur and events of only infinitesimal likelihood practically never occur. This all in fact accords with the mathematical laws of chance!

Another important factor in considering whether some unlikely event will occur is working out how many opportunities it has of occurring. A one in fourteen million chances event (e.g. winning the British national lottery) is very unlikely to occur in any one instance but if one has a million goes (or opportunities) at it, the chances are transformed into a distinct possibility. Similarly a train is very unlikely to be derailed on any one journey but if it makes very many journeys then it becomes a distinct possibility (albeit not a probability) that it will eventually be derailed. However god does not have multiple chances, not even multiple infinitesimal chances, of existing. There is only one Universe here for an entity to be God over and any potential God in the Universe is only one of a practically infinite number of entities of whom at most one may be God. So the chance of an entity being God (including combining, say, omnipotence with supreme goodness) is only one in practically infinity chances.

So mathematical chance does apply though one has to take careful account of precise likelihood (e.g. whether distinctly possible or almost impossible) and of the number of chances available. As a potential God does not (unlike a train in its possibilities of crashing) have multiple chances of occurring and also has at best an infinitesimal chance of existing, it has no real hope of overcoming the forces of mathematical unlikelihood and existing. In contrast to many things that occur the possibility of God existing is not just handicapped but pretty well obliterated by the forces of mathematical chance. At that level of mathematical unlikelihood very, very little, insignificantly little, can overcome the forces of Mathematics – and actually nevertheless occur or exist. Therefore unlike in instances where mathematical forces (or chances) are a lot weaker, mathematical considerations do indeed in reality prevent the possibility of God existing!

(vi) Rare Events Can Be Especially Significant

The possible objection here is that not only do rare events sometimes occur, but also when they do occur they can frequently or at any rate disproportionately frequently be of overwhelming significance. For instance a train might be unlikely to crash but if it does crash it can be an event of enormous significance and to say the least of disproportionate significance compared to its chances of occurring. One can argue that the same applies to each one of us – it was extremely unlikely that the individual sperm which produced us would win the struggle to come to life but as it did so against all the odds that unlikely triumph of that sperm was of huge significance to each of us!

I think there are some fallacies here. In some cases an event such as one's particular sperm winning the race to fertilise an egg may perhaps not be as generally significant as it seems to us. After all if one's sperm did not win this race and lead to our birth perhaps some other sperm would have won that race and populated the world with some other human (not in the scheme of things overwhelmingly different to us at least in its human essentials). This may have made an enormous difference to us but maybe not such a difference to the world at large!

However more fundamentally this objection confuses 'the significance of something' with 'the actual chance of that something occurring.' Nobody denies that God if he existed would (at least potentially) be of considerable significance – what is denied is there is any real chance of God existing in the first place! If something does not or practically cannot exist it cannot be of any real significance in any event. That is very different to something actually existing and being of significance when of course more account should be taken of its existence. It can even be validly argued that in some circumstances even the clear possibility of a significant event such as a large asteroid hitting the Earth ought to be taken seriously into account even if there is a strong chance it will not actually occur while humans live on the Earth! However that surely and logically does not apply in the case of something that has no real (or only an infinitesimal) chance of existing even if it would be significant in the practically impossible event of it existing. After all it would in effect just be a waste of everybody's time and effort to devote significant attention to a merely hypothetical possibility that has no significant or realistic chance of ever existing at all! So my response to this objection is that it does not matter how significant a thing may be if it hypothetically were to exist when in reality there is no significant nor real chance of it existing at all.

(vii) This Is No Disproof?

I can foresee here a possible objection that even if it is admitted that God is so incredibly improbable a proposition that there is only the most infinitesimal chance that he exists, that still does not amount to an actual disproof of God's existence.

In one sense, albeit in an insignificant sense, this objection may be valid inasmuch as the Aggregate Of Qualities Argument against the existence of God is not a proof of the absolute physical impossibility of God existing – indeed it still allows an infinitesimal, albeit insignificant chance that God does actually exist. But in the actual real world there comes a time when overwhelming probability becomes synonymous with reality or proof or disproof. Obviously this is not so when the chances of a phenomenon are one in three, not even one in thirty, but it is beginning to approach at one in three hundred and for most people it has come at one in three thousand or at any rate at one in thirty thousand. At one in three hundred thousand it is getting ridiculous and at one in three million there is to most intents and purposes no difference between no chance, nought in three million and one in three million. Among countless millions, or indeed countless millions of millions, a single mere chance (in contrast to an actual rare occurrence!) in those countless millions of millions of being wrong cannot reasonably in any significant practical sense be said to negate a proof. Such a remote possibility is not statistically significant and would normally be completely discounted in statistical terms. We have in reality long since reached a stage of probability concerning God's non-existence which is as good as and as strong as proof. Few, if any, of our items of knowledge, settled knowledge, apply to that degree of certainty. Genetic fingerprints are not that reliable; indeed even ordinary fingerprinting is not that reliable. Photographs are not that reliable, nor is geographical measurement. Evolutionary laws are not proved to that degree – not even what are called the laws of Chemistry and Physics are established to that degree. Indeed if we insisted for our knowledge upon that degree of certainty we would know practically nothing and get practically nowhere. There comes a point where we have to accept and do accept an overwhelming degree of probability as an established truth – and that point is well before one comes to the one chance in countless millions to which this aggregate of qualities argument against the existence of God is valid.

So the aggregate of qualities argument against God's existence may not strictly speaking quite be an absolute disproof of God's existence. However because of its sheer overwhelming weight of probability, it has got to a stage where it is as good as and akin in practical terms to any other disproof. So if the argumentation is valid The Aggregate Of Qualities Argument does not fail in its mission to disprove God's existence because of the arithmetic of the process.

So none of these seven types of objection to The Aggregate Of Qualities Argument damages the essential validity of the argument. All that ought to be conceded to objectors after analysing possible objections to this argument are two things. First, like most other proofs or disproofs in life it is not an absolute disproof. Yet it falls so little short of being an absolute disproof as not to matter. Secondly, some of God's essential qualities might possibly tend to coalesce. Yet there are sufficient entirely non-coalescent qualities for the chance of God existing still to be one in countless billions, that is so absolutely infinitesimal that it can in statistical terms safely be discounted. Therefore the core of this argument (that because of the inherent unlikelihood of unique yet disparate qualities combining in one entity, God, there is effectively no chance in statistical terms that God exists) remains valid, even after considering the likely objections that may be raised.

E. The Argument In Perspective

It is certainly a novel approach of mine to look at the possible existence of God in statistical terms based on the chances of his various unique qualities clustering together within one individual entity. Even the arguments concerning the improbability of any individual version of belief in God, though statistical in their tenor, have not been developed as thoroughly in statistical terms as my argument into the realms of an infinitesimal chance effectively in practical terms being the equivalent to no chance. What an unusual insight this is! But does it work? Well, let us look at the various logical stages of the argument, stage by stage.

I cannot see any credible way of disputing the first premise or stage of this argument, which is that God must have several remarkable qualities such as supreme goodness, omnipotence and immortality if he is to be God. Nor can I see any feasible quarrel with the second premise or stage of this argument, that each of these qualities may well not exist in any entity and if they do exist, they exist but rarely or uniquely. The third stage of the argument that it is highly unlikely for any one of these qualities to exist in one particular entity follows entirely naturally and logically from the second premise.

The fourth stage of this argument, that there is an infinitesimal chance that any entity might possess the combination of even two of these qualities let alone all of them, seems on the surface to follow naturally from the third stage. Yet it is potentially the weakest link in the argument and is open to challenges. Although the hypothetical objection that there is any definitive evidence we finite mortals can obtain that an entity actually possesses a combination of these qualities can be discounted, we must consider the possibility that these qualities are ultimately inherently related. As I suggested when considering this point in Section D(iii), I think the qualities should be categorised into spheres such as power qualities, moral values and endurability. While I concede that those qualities which are in the same sphere (such as power) may be inherently related (although not identical and indeed potentially separable) to other qualities within that same sphere, I do not consider that the spheres themselves are inherently related. For instance I understand 'power' to be one thing and 'values' to be another thing, 'values' relating to one's inherent nature, not to one's power to make oneself the best entity. I along with Peter Abelard (1079-1142) and Heloise (c1100-c1163) and others believe that moral values must relate primarily to one's original intentions rather than to one's sheer ability to fulfil one's intentions.

(Heloise wrote – 'It is not so much what things are done as the spirit in which they are done that we must consider.' Letter 5, see Penguin Classics, The Letters Of Abelard And Heloise. I agree.) Therefore any entity's moral worth is accordingly independent from and separate from its power. But just suppose – which I believe to be definitely wrong – in the worst case for this argument it were possible for an omnipotent being to make itself supremely good (just as it is possible for us to 'improve' ourselves by learning a foreign language). Even if supreme goodness was not a matter of one's nature or one's intent, we should still see that the possibility of a monotheistic God existing is still remote. First of all an omnipotent entity would actually have to exist although there might well be no omnipotent entity. Secondly, that omnipotent entity would have to actually choose to be supremely good, even if it could so choose, and it might well not choose to be supremely good: after all what reason would it have to do so? Thirdly, that omnipotent entity would also have to have or acquire all the other characteristics that God must necessarily have. So even in this worst case scenario for this argument the possibility that God exists is still statistically remote because it still cannot be said that these remarkable qualities must necessarily exist, let alone coexist. The most that can then be argued is that if an omnipotent entity exists (which is itself doubtful) all the other qualities might be willed or chosen to coexist (if indeed such qualities can be chosen or conjured up rather than merely exist, or not exist, as natural phenomena). Therefore even in this worst case scenario for this argument God must rationally on the overwhelming balance of probabilities be assumed not to exist. However I do not concede this worst case scenario is true since for instance I think supreme goodness is a natural quality, not a chosen quality. So I do not think it proper to concede that the existence of God is merely a highly unlikely chance rather than an absolutely infinitesimal chance.

The final stage of this argument is to state that for statistical and indeed for all practical purposes an absolutely infinitesimal chance is equivalent to no chance at all. This is generally indisputable in statistical terms and so in practical terms is fair comment. This applies in respect of every and any entity, even a potential God. So we certainly cannot properly nor reasonably base religious belief upon merely an infinitesimal chance that it may be true without even any logically clear and significant indication that it is true. We must assume, if we are to assume anything, that what is statistically overwhelmingly likely is indeed true.

So I commend The Aggregate Of Qualities Argument against the existence of God as sensible in its approach and correct in its conclusion. Certainly the approach of seeing God not merely as a thing but as a combination of remarkable and often unique qualities rolled into one is correct. I think because of the inherently different nature of some of these unique qualities that this argument properly shows that there is only an infinitesimal chance that God exists. Therefore to all intents and purposes God does not exist. Admittedly if it is thought – which I dispute – that all these qualities, including supreme goodness, may arise out of God's ability to will (omnipotence) then this argument is weakened. Yet even then this argument still shows that it is highly unlikely God exists (because it is unlikely that some such properties as immortality can be willed by anything and second there is an omnipotent entity in the first place and in the third place that an omnipotent entity should actually choose to will all the various other qualities, including supreme goodness).

I therefore conclude that this form of statistical argument against God's existence is valid. I can see no valid objection either to the validity of looking at matters from a statistical approach or to the notion that this view of things makes the existence of God very unlikely in statistical terms. The only real scope for dispute is the matter of just how unlikely God's existence actually is. Such debate arises mainly from the question how far God's various essential qualities are genuinely inherently different qualities and how far they may be coalescent qualities. Yet in any event even on the most hostile defensible view of this argument, this argument does validly lead to the conclusion that it is far more likely that God does not exist than that God does exist. Therefore God should not be believed in. I myself argue that this argument is valid to the full extent of stating that there is only an infinitesimal chance of God existing because some of God's essential yet unique qualities are genuinely inherently unconnected in their nature. However we are perhaps discussing here merely a difference of emphasis. On either view, whether it is merely unlikely that God exists or whether there is only an infinitesimal chance that God exists it is illogical and unreasonable to believe in (let alone worship) the existence of God. So this argument certainly does succeed in logically showing that humans cannot rationally nor sensibly believe in the existence of a monotheistic God.

CHAPTER 2

The Man And God Comprehension Gulf Argument

A. Prologue

This is essentially an argument that people cannot logically believe in the existence of God because no person can have the capacity to identify God even if God did exist. There is a comprehension gulf between a potential God and Man which mankind is incapable of bridging. If people do try to assert the existence of God they are inevitably caught in a comprehension paradox – 'God is beyond human comprehension. I comprehend that it is God that exists.' Of course if God is beyond human comprehension, one cannot properly comprehend that God exists. This argument is intended to prove that a monotheistic God would actually be beyond human comprehension and so would be unidentifiable by humans.

This problem people may have in identifying at least any particular version of God is actually a longstanding problem. In fact people in previous polytheistic societies (where there were a variety of Gods and Gods were not necessarily good, merely very powerful) were more aware of this problem than are modern people. For instance in the ancient Greek myths Gods were liable to disguise themselves (as exemplified by Ares in Book V of Homer's Iliad and by Dionysus in The Bacchae by the Greek playwright Euripides). Ancient Greek Gods supposedly often appeared in disguise in human form. That made their identification difficult or even impossible for humans before they manifested themselves rather more clearly (in apparent terms at least), usually through the visible exercise of their power. Hinduism also contains stories about Gods appearing in various guises and disguises that make their identification by humans difficult. Even the Jewish God, Jehovah, was very concerned in the Bible's Old Testament to be identified by people as the only authentic God. In the famous Ten Commandments (Exodus Chapter 20), Jehovah's very first commandment was "You shall have no other gods before me." This apparent God (Jehovah) cruelly vented his anger even upon his chosen people for temporarily deserting him and recognising or creating instead another apparent rival God (Exodus Chapter 32) in the form of a golden calf. The Bible states, 'And the LORD plagued the people because they made the calf.'

Some people, including some religious people, particularly mystics, have affirmed that God is indeed beyond human comprehension. However, people have generally failed to see the logical corollary that if the concept of God is beyond human comprehension people cannot know that God exists and therefore people should not believe in the existence of God. David Hume (1711-1776) was one person who understood that God may be beyond human comprehension. Hume put this point into the speech of Philo in Part I of his Dialogues Concerning Natural Religion – '... when we look beyond human affairs and the properties of the surrounding bodies; when we carry our speculations into the two eternities, before and after the present state of things, into the creation and formation of the Universe; the existence and properties of spirits; the powers and operations of one universal Spirit existing without beginning and without end, omnipotent, omniscient, immutable, infinite and incomprehensible. We must be far removed from the smallest tendency to scepticism not to be apprehensive that we have got here quite beyond the reach of our faculties. So long as we confine our speculations to trade, or morals, or politics, or criticism, we make appeals, every moment, to common sense and experience, which strengthen our philosophical conclusions and remove (at least in part) the suspicion, which we so justly entertain with regard to every reasoning, that is very subtle and refined. But in theological reasonings, we have not this advantage; while at the same time we are employed upon objects which, we must be sensible, are too large for our grasp.' Yet even Hume himself did not assert that that means belief in God is therefore irrational and logically indefensible (as it is) because no kind of monotheistic God can ever be identified by humans. Indeed it is not known for certain whether Hume himself was an atheist. In fact it seems that nobody up to now, certainly nobody prominent, has even pointed out the sheer absurdity of human incomprehension of God combining with any belief in God. Nobody yet has expressed this combination as a paradox, what I call The Comprehension Paradox – 'God is beyond human comprehension. I comprehend that it is God that exists.' Therefore though some others have seen that a potential God would indeed be beyond human comprehension, nobody before me has seemingly gone on to see this has the logical corollary that God therefore cannot be identified by humans and should not be believed in by humans. This fully developed argument it seems is original to myself.

B. Summary Of The Argument

1. Man is finite (in time, space and power etc).

2. God if he exists is infinite (in time, space and power etc).

3. Therefore mankind cannot possibly recognise God or even know that God exists.

C. Explaining The Argument

The fundamental point in this argument is that as we humans see only a very small part of the picture of the Universe we cannot be sure about the nature of the whole Universe. In point of fact we cannot even be sure we are actually seeing accurately and correctly (without distortion) the part of the Universe we appear to be able to see. Yet even if we observe our part of the Universe, our small part of the whole picture, reasonably accurately we cannot be sure what the whole Universe is like.

A good (though hardly adequate in scale) analogy is with a jigsaw. Once just a few pieces of a vast jigsaw have been put together we still cannot be sure what the whole vast jigsaw picture would comprise. Say for argument's sake the jigsaw is a picture of the whole surface of the Earth, and all that we can see is a couple of square miles of uninhabited desert. Assume we had no other knowledge nor experience of the phenomena (the Earth's surface) beyond that. We could not then tell from that that a fuller picture of the surface of the Earth would also feature forests, seas, cities, snow capped mountains, Arctic regions and many other things absent from that relatively small patch of desert.

Likewise, in more abstract terms we cannot from our limited existence in time and space and indeed from our limited mental capabilities tell what might or might not lie far beyond our experience in space and time. So we humans would be foolish to make any definitive pronouncement unsubstantiated by Logic of what may exist in the totality of Space and Time. Indeed given our limited perspective and abilities we could even be unwise to make many definitive pronouncements about the underlying reality of the phenomena we appear to see and experience.

Relating all this to God's existence, the obstacles for us are that we are mortal but God would be immortal, we are finite but God would be infinite and we are limited in capacity but God would be unlimited in capacity. It is simply not possible for any entity that is mortal like we humans are to know for sure that some other entity is immortal. How could we humans recognise God because how can we humans be sure it will not die sometime after we ourselves die? Furthermore how can we humans even be sure that it has lived for all eternity before our own birth, indeed before even the formation of our planet? It is also simply not possible for any entity like us humans that is confined to a relatively small area of Space to know what lies out in the far reaches of Space. So we humans cannot possibly know whether an apparent God is genuinely God over all Space or just a local potentate over our region of Space with no control over the outer reaches of Space. For all we humans know a local God-like potentate might even be subject to destruction by an even greater potentate journeying from the depths of outer Space into our more local region of Space! Furthermore it is simply not possible for any entity like us humans that is limited in intelligence and brainpower to know for sure that some other entity is unlimited in intelligence and at the apex of wisdom. How could we humans even identify an entity of supreme intelligence and be entirely sure that there is not somewhere else another entity of even greater intelligence? It is even worse than a Neanderthal Man having to distinguish between the intellects of Isaac Newton and Albert Einstein – and then having to predict whether and in what ways the intellect of Einstein might in future be surpassed by another person! So how can any mortal, finite, limited entity possibly identify or properly even assert the existence of any immortal, infinite and unlimited entity such as a monotheistic God would have to be? How can any human therefore identify any entity as God? The answer has to be that within the standards of Logic humans can neither recognise any particular entity as God nor know in general that God exists.

A crucial illustration of this comes in our inevitable inability (given our limited scope and powers) to distinguish what may just be a powerful daemon (albeit a daemon proclaiming falsely to us that it is God) from a genuine God. If such a daemon is much longer lived (although perhaps eventually doomed to die), much more extensive and much more powerful than us it may well be able to deceive us into believing it is a truly existing immortal, infinite and omnipotent entity! This is a crucially important point, especially as the Universe might feature very many such powerful daemons but could not feature more than one real God. So any such entity we may encounter is indeed far more likely to be a powerful daemon than a genuine God. This example shows that given our mortal human limitations we cannot possibly tell the difference between a seemingly benevolent very powerful daemon and a real God (if such exists). In fact there is nothing whatsoever that could conceivably constitute for humans positive evidence of God's existence. This is because there is nothing, no evidence (and no demonstrations of power, knowledge, goodness, miracles or whatever) that could not be produced in front of us by a very powerful yet deceptive daemon rather than by a genuine God. So because of our limitations we humans could not properly ever even identify or recognise God (and distinguish it from a possible daemon) even if we ever actually encountered God. In this connexion there are two kinds of things we might still be able to do. One thing is to work out through evidence (such as the death or impotence or errors of an entity) that some particular entity is not God. The other thing we might possibly be able to do, as I am elsewhere attempting to do, is to prove through logic that God cannot exist at all.

The comprehension, mortality and power gulf between us and a potential God is so great that we humans lack, inevitably lack, the means to identify God even if God exists. So as we cannot properly identify God inevitably we are not and can never be in a position rationally to believe in any monotheistic God. Therefore on that basis alone the only rational course for us would be to abstain from any belief in God and abstain from any religion.

D. Possible Objections To The Argument

Now let us consider possible objections to this argument. However it is not even possible to argue with the first premise of this argument, against the facts that humans are mortal, limited in their scope and indeed only know much about a very small part of the Universe. Nor of course is it possible to argue with the second premise of this argument, that God would necessarily have to be immortal and infinite in scope. So the basic premises of this argument are really beyond dispute. However let us look at what seemingly plausible objections might be conjured up.

(i) Faith Or Mysticism Overcomes This Argument

Of course many religious apologists would willingly admit that God is beyond the scope of our human comprehension. Yet they would claim that Man's relationship with God must transcend our rational faculties and be based on faith, or according to some upon mystical experience of God.

However neither faith nor mysticism can overcome this argument. Neither faith nor mysticism can make the mortal immortal, the impotent omnipotent or the limited unlimited. So the gulf between a possible God and us, between the immortal and the mortal, between the unlimited and the limited, remains and so does the impossibility of the mortal being able to identify what is immortal and the impossibility of what is finite being able to identify what is infinite. Even if there were a different method of confirming knowledge than the rational method (which I dispute and certainly dispute in the case of sheer irrational faith or mysticism) these same problems would remain. The gulf between a potential God and us humans would remain and so the problem of humans being logically unable to identify a genuine God which is an insuperable problem for us humans would still remain.

(ii) Everyday Life Is Based On Trust Without Such Scepticism

Some people might object that the search for certain proof about our feelings concerning God is so much pedantic nonsense because that just does not correspond with how we live our lives in other respects. Elsewhere we are generally content to take things on trust. We trust our senses and we trust intellectual authority. We don't start intellectualising about whether our father exists, or whether a particular man is our father but we just accept the situation as we see it and as we are told it is and we live our lives accordingly. Likewise when we cross the road we don't start intellectualising over whether the cars we see exist as cars in reality, we just assume they do and consequently take care to avoid being hit by them. Even in the sciences we accept on trust many items of knowledge. We even accept 'knowledge' in Physics and Astronomy that may be based upon far fetched extrapolations into Space and Time that are so far beyond our experience and indeed are so abstruse that we personally will never and indeed never can experience them.

This objection, even if tempting, is not valid. Undoubtedly people do generally accept things on the evidence of their senses and on trust in everyday life. However although our senses are adequate for the identification of everyday things (at least to the extent of assuming their existence as reasonable working hypotheses) for everyday life, our senses are not adequate for the identification of God. For a start in everyday life we are helped in identification by similarities with other entities whereas God would necessarily be unique. Even more importantly whereas everyday things such as cars and other people are also limited, finite and temporary in the way we are, God's essential characteristics include being omnipotent, omniscient and eternal – it is these essential qualities of God that we cannot possibly recognise because we humans are not competent physically or mentally to do so. Nor should we accept God's existence even as a reasonable hypothesis because that would need far more extensive evidence than could be available to us. Furthermore sundry other explanations such as powerful daemons are at least as likely if not more likely than God to explain the evidence available to us. As for the point that we go beyond our senses in accepting the extrapolations entailed in physical and astronomical theories as reality, it should be noted that those theories and the alleged facts derived from them are not accepted arbitrarily nor completely unevidenced nor absolutely (as God would be). Moreover such scientific theories are only accepted as provisional theories until, if ever, they are disproved or until some more plausible theory to explain our observations arises at which time that part of Science will be revised to accommodate the new information or theory then available.

(iii) Our Doubt Is Not A Valid Argument Against God

It is sometimes claimed that doubting is not a valid form of argument. Some people say we must doubt the validity of our doubting and indeed of an argument based upon our ignorance. Some people say doubting is just such a comprehensive destroyer of knowledge that it would mean we can never know anything.

The objection that doubting is not a valid activity in argumentation because you may doubt your doubts is invalid. There is such a thing as a legitimate doubt and indeed a legitimate ignorance or incomprehension. We cannot properly doubt or deny that a realm of ignorance arises when a finite, mortal entity attempts to recognise an entity of another type that is infinite and immortal. We cannot properly dismiss the unbridgeable chasm that arises for the mortal and finite entity between the mortal and the immortal and between the finite and the infinite. We cannot make that unbridgeable chasm disappear by suggesting there is any doubt about that chasm. Nor can the inevitable ignorance of the infinite by the finite be irrelevant to thinking finite entities.

As for the point that if you start doubting things, all possible knowledge just disintegrates into one large and inconclusive doubt about all things, that is not entirely valid either. The truth of the matter is that it is generally far easier to disprove a theory than to prove a theory. This applies particularly when you see only part of a picture. For instance imagine you have fitted together only a few pieces of a vast jigsaw puzzle, perhaps of the surface of the Earth, and these pieces comprise desert. That is sufficient to indicate that not all the surface of the Earth can be sea but it is insufficient to accurately extrapolate to the theory that the whole surface of the Earth consists of desert. Likewise from our limited human perspective we can often see clearly and without legitimate doubt what cannot be the case, even if we cannot be sure of what actually is the case. Yet, more basically, along the lines of René Descartes (1596-1650), because we do have experiences we can be certain that something actually exists and something is happening within the Universe. There are some things therefore which we cannot logically be in doubt of.

(iv) This Is An Argument About Human Incapacity, Not About God's Existence

The objection here is that this whole comprehension gulf argument really has nothing to do with whether God exists or not. It is only about whether we humans can discover God. To state that we cannot discover God, as this argument attempts to prove, is different to demonstrating that God does not exist. An analogy is that there is a big difference between asserting that European men before Christopher Columbus could not discover America and asserting that America did not then exist. That European men could not then discover America has nothing to do with whether America actually existed or not. Similarly that men cannot discover nor properly identify God has nothing to do with whether God exists or not. So though we might demonstrate by this argument that people cannot be sure that God exists, this argument does not prove that God does not exist.

I suspect some people might like to counter this objection by insisting that it is an essential characteristic of a monotheistic God that he can be known by us and can communicate with us. However I think, that given it is impossible for the mortal to be sure of the immortal and for the finite to be sure of the infinite, that would be asking for the impossible. Yet it is generally not supposed to be one of God's characteristics that he accomplishes what is logically impossible. Therefore I refrain from arguing this.

So the point that the comprehension gulf argument is an argument that shows we are unable to demonstrate the existence of God rather than an argument that shows God does not exist is valid. However even so all religions are still undermined by this argument irrespective of whether God actually exists. Sensible people would not worship a possible entity whose real existence (if such there is) they are necessarily incapable of determining, let alone identifying.

So in conclusion I myself can see no valid objection to this argument so long as one accepts that this is an argument that God cannot be identified nor even shown to exist rather than an argument absolutely disproving the existence of God. However it is not logical nor proper to believe in or hypothecate the existence of an entity whose existence it is inevitably beyond our scope to substantiate.

Furthermore it is hard to envisage that there could be a valid objection to this argument since its two premises are indisputably and inevitably true and the conclusion follows logically from the premises. It is for instance only logical that a mortal cannot tell whether a supposedly immortal entity will die after it (the mortal entity) is dead. So mortals can neither identify any entity as God nor know (assuming it was logically feasible for God to exist) whether God actually does exist.

E. The Argument In Perspective

In evaluating The Man And God Comprehension Gulf Argument the question is not really whether the argument is valid but rather what the argument really amounts to.

There can be no disputing that Man is a finite entity, finite in time, space and power and that this argument's first premise is true. That is self evident. There can also be no question that if God exists, God would have to be infinite, infinite in time, space and power or else he would not be God. So the second premise is clearly true. Also the conclusion that humans because of their limitations cannot recognise an infinite god follows logically from the premises and is undoubtedly correct. Nor crucially could humans distinguish god from an entity, a seemingly good daemon, that is far more powerful than humans but far less powerful than a real god would be.

So the significant questions are what does this valid argument amount to and where does it leave us? It must be admitted that this argument is essentially an argument concerning human limitations and human ignorance and it does not actually absolutely prove or disprove the existence of God. However what it does prove is that we humans could never possibly recognise God. We can of course recognise that a cruel, mortal entity is not God and we can know that if the world is unnecessarily pernicious God could hardly have created or tolerated it. But on the other hand we can never positively identify God. For instance as we are not immortal we can never distinguish a sufficiently powerful daemon (or 'force') that might in due course die from an eternal God because we will simply never live long enough to confirm that an entity will not die. Furthermore this argument does show that all people who assert the existence of God are necessarily in the paradoxical and illogical and thus unsustainable position of asserting The Comprehension Paradox – i.e. 'God is beyond human comprehension: I comprehend that God exists.' Since all people are necessarily finite and God would necessarily have to be infinite, theists assert the existence of God without ever being properly able to identify anything as God. So this argument shows we cannot prove the existence of God at least if there is any alternative at all (even the sheer chance assemblage of things, let alone accelerated evolution) to God existing. (One might say that if God must necessarily exist and there were no logical alternative to that, this argument would not prove God cannot exist, just that we humans could not recognise God. However if there is any logically feasible alternative to God existing, which there clearly is, we would not be able to show that God does exist.) However this argument proves we humans could not in any case identify any entity as God.

This argument of course does not preclude the possibility that we might show that God is a logically impossible concept and so disprove the possibility of God existing. After all seeing a desert does not prove that the whole world is desert but it does disprove the notion that the whole world's surface is sea. Likewise we may not see God but we may see so much suffering as to be sure God cannot exist. Though we cannot prove that any entity is immortal we may still be able to disprove that any entity is omniscient. We may still be able to prove that irrespective of whether any entity is immortal, God cannot exist because no entity can logically have some of the other divine qualities. So this Man And God Comprehension Gulf Argument closes the door to identifying God but it does not remove the possibility of absolutely disproving the existence of God.

So in conclusion, although The God And Man Comprehension Gulf Argument does not absolutely disprove the existence of God, it is a significant argument because it shows that God even if he exists must logically necessarily be far beyond human capacity for identification. As we humans must properly be guided by Logic (as we have no other consistent and reliable guide by which to progress) we cannot properly believe in (still less worship) a God that even if it existed would be unidentifiable by us humans. So we humans cannot be blamed (even by a potential God!) for not believing in God when we cannot possibly find sufficient evidence to justify such a belief! In such circumstances it is only proper for people not actually to believe in any god.

The 'God Has No Explanatory Value' Argument

A. Prologue

This is an argument that combines two strands, neither of them original, into an original argument against belief in the existence of God. It synthesises a refusal to accept without evidence an artificial and indeed unwarranted answer to the question of original cause with Occam's Razor Law (particularly in relation to what in scientific or logical terms should be incorporated into positive human belief). In general in scientific or existential terms theories are only to be believed in if they have some 'explanatory value'. However this argument shows that God has no genuine explanatory value.

Let us start with the simplest approach to this argument. The question who created God occurs readily to children and sometimes even to adults when they are told that God created the world but that question is never properly answered. This question ('who created God?') is so simple and occurs so readily that its age and first use is unrecorded and is probably as old as the notion of God as Creator. Presumably because this question cannot be answered satisfactorily it is usually dismissed contemptuously by theists as childish, facile and at best missing the point. It is certainly not responded to seriously by theists. This in turn has discouraged most non-theists from treating it seriously, indeed with the serious attention it actually merits. The main response that seems to occur to theists is that being the ultimate Creator is part of the very definition of God and so by definition God himself is an uncaused cause and could not himself have been created. Yet that is only playing with words and does not offer any compelling, nor even reasonable reason why our hypothetical creator should not himself have been created by a yet more powerful entity than even it. After all if every question could be answered by just postulating a definitional answer then life would be simple but that is not the reality of things! Furthermore the postulation that our own hypothetical Creator is not himself created is not merely a matter of verbal definition but of genuine substance. Indeed the very arguments used to postulate a Creator – intelligence and order in the world – would suggest that our Creator being cleverer and even more complex than us is himself even more in need of a Creator than we humans are! So theists have succeeded not in answering but in generally mocking out of consideration a very pertinent and relevant question by which the whole concept of God is properly undermined! Despite this the question who created God has occasionally been asked not just by children but also by informed adults. The ancient Indian Carvakas (a materialist school of philosophy) probably as far back as the sixth century BC argued that the supposed existence of a Creator implies a Metacreator and so on. This point does not seem to have been answered then or now. Others, including Ludwig Feuerbach (1804-1872) and David Hume (1711-1776) have in effect questioned the explanatory usefulness of postulating the existence of God. Feuerbach wrote in Chapter XIX of his book The Essence Of Christianity, 'Religion denies, repudiates chance, making everything dependent on God, explaining everything by means of him; but this denial is only apparent; it merely gives chance the name of divine sovereignty. For the divine will, which on incomprehensible grounds for incomprehensible reasons, that is, speaking plainly, out of groundless, absolute arbitrariness, out of divine caprice, as it were, determines or predestines some to evil and misery, others to good and happiness, has not a single positive characteristic to distinguish it from the power of chance.' Hume under the cloak of a character, Philo, in Part IV of Dialogues Concerning Natural Religion was also critical – 'Naturalists, indeed, very justly explain particular effects by more general causes; though these general causes themselves should remain in the end totally inexplicable: But they never surely thought it satisfactory to explain a particular effect by a particular cause which was no more to be accounted for than the effect itself.'

It is not only problems with the creative quality of God but also the lack of apparent reason for separating God from Nature itself that damages the usefulness or explanatory value of the God concept. The fundamental problem theists encounter and are unable to overcome is that there is no valid reason for postulating God and then stopping one's postulations when one has got to God. There is generally no adequate reason for postulating the existence of God in the first place. But once one has postulated God there is no less reason (indeed greater reason since God being greater than us is even more in need of explanation than we are) for postulating an ever greater series of Gods such as Supergod, God of the Gods, etc, etc to infinity which of course is incompatible with <u>mono</u>theism! So in intellectual terms a journey to the concept of God cannot really be justified in the first place, but once God has been postulated an infinite journey to an ever greater sequence of Gods cannot properly be prevented either. Indeed if one has (mistakenly!) accepted the reason for the original resort to God as being valid, the reasons for regressing ever further along a route to ever greater Gods are even more compelling. In practice it is only a combination of human psychological unwillingness to go down that route and an invalid sleight of words that is used, incorrectly used, by theists that usually prevents that infinite regress!

The other part of this argument is the introduction of the principles of Occam's Razor and 'explanatory value' in relation to belief in God. William of Occam (c1285-1349) was an English, Franciscan medieval thinker who advocated a logical principle of ontological economy that 'entities are not to be multiplied beyond necessity'. That means that an entity or thing is only to be hypothesised if it contributes materially towards an explanation of phenomena. Occam himself being a Franciscan did not apply his own principle to God. However in the case of God this must mean that God ought only to be hypothesised as a possible concept if hypothesising God actually really explains anything rather than just allows exactly the same question to be validly asked in relation to God as in relation to the original phenomenon. For instance to answer the question who created the Universe by postulating the existence of God does not really answer the question because exactly the same question can be asked in relation to God, namely who created God. Thus according to Occam's Razor principle the hypothecation of God is multiplying entities because it is adding the entity of God without answering the essential question of ultimate creation. So there is here a multiplication of entities beyond necessity which according to Occam (and Occam was correct in this) ought as a logical principle to be avoided. In other words, and in more modern words, a theory ought to have explanatory value if it is to be entertained. But the theory that God exists and created the Universe has no real explanatory value in relation to the ultimate origin of the Universe because it still leaves unexplained the question of how God himself came to exist – so it does not answer the essential question about the ultimate origin of the whole Universe. Indeed the postulation of God only complicates things. It adds an unwarranted stage and another though unwarranted and unevidenced element to the problem without actually solving (or helping to solve) the problem about how things were originally created or came to exist as they are. Therefore the postulation that God exists would not be considered plausible, let alone satisfactory, as a scientific theory because it is unevidenced and ultimately contributes nothing to explanation. It merely adds the complication of extrapolating an extra stage to the mystery we set out to solve.

Neither the question who created God nor Occam's Razor Law is original to myself. The originality I can claim in this particular argument is in combining the two concepts and in generally questioning 'the explanatory value' of the concept of God. Furthermore as (unlike Occam or previous generations) we live in a scientific age, I am able to formulate the argument in terms of the logic of scientific method. So I can state that a theory that is neither credibly evidenced nor has any real explanatory value should not be adopted nor believed in (even provisionally) as a hypothesis or theory because it falls far short of what is acceptable as a scientific theory. Therefore in logical and scientific terms in the absence of credible supporting evidence or explanatory value the existence of God should not even be postulated as a hypothesis, let alone believed in by anybody sensible.

B. Summary Of The Argument

1. God if he exists must be the ultimate being and provide the answer to all our ultimate questions – otherwise he is not really God.

2. Yet even supposing as a hypothesis that God exists the questions that God was supposed to finally answer still remain (though in some cases God is substituted in the question for the Universe).

3. Therefore hypothesising God's existence is only unnecessarily adding an extra stage to such problems and has no real explanatory value.

4. Therefore according to Logic (Occam's Razor Law – 'that entities are not to be multiplied beyond necessity') we should not postulate God's existence and there is no adequate reason to suppose that God exists.

5. Therefore we should suppose that God does not exist.

C. Explaining The Argument

I can explain this argument in the following way.

Essentially, this argument is that God is in logical terms a valueless extra complication (and therefore a further obstacle) to understanding things. What cosmic problem does God really help us solve? None. 'God is eternal.' Well, so might the Universe be. 'God is absolute good.' What in any event is absolute good? – I think it is in essence and in definition independent of God. 'God provides a purpose to life.' How can God conceivably add a purpose to life that was not previously there? What exactly is that purpose? – if we do not know it might as well not exist (and if it is merely the circular purpose of worshipping God, what indeed is the purpose of that?). If you ask how did the Universe arise, the answer for theists is, of course, God created it. But how did God arise? Well, God has always existed. But, why then, has the Universe not always existed? Thus God can be cut out as an unnecessary extra. Poor God, always being cut out as an unnecessary extra which contributes nothing to understanding except complication. God is no more than a valueless extra intermediary stage in explanation. Yet we live in a world whose rational ethos (in accordance with Occam's Razor Law – i.e. 'entities are not to be multiplied beyond necessity') is to adopt the simplest solution which will explain all the phenomena, and God is never that. God can answer no questions which cannot be answered in similar terms without him whether the questions are about absolute goodness, purpose or our genesis or as far as I can see about anything else. So God contributes nothing except a valueless extra stage to the answer of any universal questions. So God has no explanatory value. So in the absence of any compelling reason to believe God exists, God should not be believed in and it is rational for us to assume that God does not exist. It should therefore be assumed by us that God does not exist.

Indeed one can actually go further and state that postulating God's existence does not merely fail to contribute to explanation but also adds extra dimensions and extra difficulties to our problems. For instance if one supposes God exists, one has then to explain not merely the sheer existence of the ultimate phenomenon but also the matter of evil in the Universe. After all evil is not irreconcilable with the simple sheer existence of the Universe but seems irreconcilable with the existence of a supremely good and omnipotent God. And of course you could also then have the difficulties of explaining such things as why different people see different Gods differently and why even religious scriptures are mutually inconsistent and so unreliable.

D. Possible Objections To The Argument

I now come to a consideration of the various possible types of objection to this argument. I can foresee six apparently credible types of objection and I shall consider them each in turn.

(i) There Is Evidence For God

The possible objection here is that this whole argument cannot apply because God is not just a theoretical postulation that can be made or unmade but rather we can know through evidence that God exists. If we could know through reliable evidence that God exists and God is not just a postulation but is an actual entity (like you or I or William Shakespeare was) it ceases to be so relevant that God apparently has no explanatory value in metaphysical terms – he just exists. Indeed in those circumstances God would actually have an explanatory value – he would be the way to explain the evidence for his existence even if he does not seem to us to ultimately explain the whole Universe.

However for this objection to be valid and correct the evidence that God exists, however derived, must be sufficiently strong to indicate that God does exist. It would not be good enough for a monotheistic God to be just one of several plausible theories (such as a combination of factors or polytheistic gods or freaks of nature) that could explain the evidence. But that is the problem for this objection. There is no actual evidence that proves the existence of God or even upon close examination indicates the existence of God is likely. Indeed it is seemingly impossible for finite humans confined to our Solar System to get conclusive evidence of the infinite or for mortals to get clear evidence of immortality into the distant past as well as immortality into all the future that is yet to come. How and upon what possible evidence could mere mortals distinguish between that which lives for a very long time (countless millions of years) and that which lives for all time? Therefore all the most plausible evidence for God might theoretically more easily be explained by a very powerful (maybe benevolent) daemon, of which there could be many in the Universe, instead of by an all-powerful God. Nor is faith in God, such as many religious apologists have, any answer. For a start faith is especially absurd when the supposed grounds for faith such as The Bible and its precepts so often self-contradict and also often contradict our modern notions of good sense and ethical behaviour. More fundamentally, faith counts for nothing in Logic as an argument or as a response to an argument. After all one may have the faith to believe in anything at all, be it imaginary or real as faith does not inherently distinguish at all between fact and fiction.

So this objection would indeed be a valid objection if there was valid and compelling evidence for the existence of God since God would then not merely be an explanatory postulate but an evidenced and concrete entity. However in the absence of such evidence this objection is not valid. There is now an absence of such evidence. Indeed I should think as we are mortals there must always inevitably be an absence of such evidence.

(ii) God's Existence Is Not Dependent On His Having Ultimate Explanatory Value For Us

This objection was expressed by David Hume (1711-1776) under the character of Cleanthes in Part IV of his Dialogues Concerning Natural Religion – 'Even in common life, if I assign a cause for any event, is it any objection that I cannot assign a cause of that cause, and answer every new question which may incessantly be started?' In other words it is no valid objection to the existence of an entity that we do not actually know the cause of that entity even if that entity is itself the cause of something else. Thus for instance if a person is seen to have set a building on fire, that is an explanation of why the fire occurred even if we do not know why the arsonist decided to set fire to the building.

Now it is perfectly true that a concrete, definitely existing entity need not have any further explanatory value other than explaining the very evidence (presumably observations of it) for its existence. But by contrast a postulated entity (especially a postulated entity that is actually supposed to have created the Universe and to explain the Universe) should have an explanatory value. The difference is that a common life entity is observed or is proved to exist but a postulated entity only has a postulated existence. Any worthwhile postulated existence is in logical terms dependent upon its being the most satisfactory and economical explanation for all the relevant phenomena that have been observed. Without such explanatory value the postulated entity would cease to be valid even as a postulation and therefore not exist even as a relevant, logically based theory. Furthermore as it is necessarily an inherent characteristic of any postulated monotheistic God that he is ultimate and can explain Universal existence, it would be even more essential to God than to other postulations that he has ultimate explanatory value.

So this objection is not valid. True, things that are gleaned from reliable empirical observation need have no explanatory value (except as a simple explanation of what is directly observed). However postulates and especially the notion of God (because of his supposed, particular, metaphysically ultimate characteristics) need to have explanatory value if they are to be at all credible and acceptable.

(iii) God Is By Definition Explanatory (The Uncaused Cause)

The objection here is that it is absurd to talk of God as not having an explanatory value when by the definition of God it is God that explains the Universe. Indeed God is the explanation that has no explanation. According to the precept of Aristotle (384-322 BC) God is the unmoved mover of the Universe, and so God is the uncaused cause of the Universe.

Well, I suppose it is possible to posit just about anything but of course mere positing does not bring anything into actual existence. For instance it is possible to posit a square circle but that does not bring a square circle into existence. In the same way it is possible to posit God (an uncaused cause of the Universe) but that too does not bring God into existence. Furthermore there is no particular reason why there should or should not be any uncaused cause and there is nothing to substantiate the notion of an uncaused cause.

Moreover even if one sidesteps the explanation for the origin of the Universe, one cannot so readily sidestep the explanation of the purpose of life. This is because the purpose of life depends not only on God providing the final explanation for the purpose of life but also upon our knowing the purpose of life which essentially we must know – otherwise as far as we are concerned in living our lives there might as well not be a purpose to life.

So this objection to the argument that God needs no explanation and that the argument can be eliminated by using the definition of God is erroneous. For a start in some ways (e.g. in the purpose to life) God's explanatory value does not only depend upon God's role but also upon our own understanding which cannot be put into just a definition of God. Furthermore the attempt to encapsulate the existence of a concept within a definition is a verbal trick for the gullible, a pretence at a solution to the question of the existence of a phenomenon, not an actual solution. It is about as intellectually useful as using pretend money (such as 'Monopoly game' money) instead of real money would be if one has no actual money to pay real debts – it is a sham that does not work. So attempting to encapsulate the existence of a posited concept just within a definition does not make that concept (here God as an uncaused cause) either credible or existent. You simply cannot bring things into real existence just by defining (or attempting to define them) into existence.

(iv) God Is Special

The objection here is that notwithstanding the logic that ordinary postulates need to have some explanatory value in order to be credible, God is so special that this requirement just does not apply to God.

Arguments might be attempted like these:

a) the consequences of not believing in God are too awful for us to follow normal principles in deciding whether God exists;

b) what applies to the material world does not apply to God;

c) God unlike anything else is unique as the ultimate reality and so the principles that apply to God are unique;

d) faith applies in respect of God whereas faith does not apply in respect of other things.

Such arguments suggest we should in the case of theology abandon the logic that is useful and applicable to everyday life (and indeed to other subjects) in favour of quasi-logic or mere intuition. However both quasi-logic and intuition are beyond the bounds both of reliable experience and also of our possible settled knowledge anyhow. Briefly, I will respond to these arguments for belief in the unproven and logically unjustifiable notion of God.

For a start it seems inappropriate that the consequences of not believing in a supremely good God that is unproven and unevidenced are so awful. Nor can one even say that it is pragmatically sensible to believe in any God because given that there are so many differing versions of God, one is very unlikely to believe in the correct version anyhow and so save oneself. In any event the personal consequences to people of not holding a theoretical belief do not determine whether that belief is correct or not.

As for the notion that God is unique and immaterial and so does not operate according to normal principles nor within the bounds of Logic, I deny that anything can exist contrary to Logic. I doubt anything can exist with that degree of inconsistency. Speaking personally, I also doubt that any real entity can exist completely immaterially. In any case we actually know nothing of the supposed alternative principles upon which God operates. That is merely human conjecture. Indeed it is irrational conjecture devised by the religious to suit the religious without any foundation at all beyond the imagination of some humans. Faith in religious terms is generally only a posh word for the reckless imaginings of ideas that cannot sensibly, let alone rationally, be believed in.

So I insist on the question, if we do not apply logic and logical principles, which we must apply in other respects of everyday life, what do we apply? There is no other coherent principle. It is part of our human condition (for which nobody, divine or otherwise, can fairly blame us) that we are bound to apply the same practical, pragmatic and seemingly effective principles to all things, however small or however great they may be. At least these rational principles work in spheres known to us whereas nothing else even does that – and so logical principles are the best that we can apply and are what we should apply. This is especially so since we can easily predict that what is contrary to Logic when Logic is correctly applied cannot work because of inherent inconsistency. We can also reasonably be confident that though what is more complex and complicated than is warranted by Logic may possibly exist, it probably does not exist and is most probably therefore fanciful theorising. So theorising about other notions (such as what an existent God – depending on what type of God it is – may do or speculating about faith or about God being different in kind to material or lesser things) than Logic is senseless. There is no proper foundation for such non-rational speculations. Indeed in human circumstances such notions outside Logic are unreasonable conjecture, conjecture which we have no sensible reason to believe is realistic.

So the notion that in epistemological and explanatory terms God (if he exists) is special should be rejected because we have no real reason to know that. Even if that were somehow true we humans have no clear experience nor guidance in the particular mode in which God is allegedly special – so we couldn't progress anywhere along that direction anyhow!

(v) God Is Metascientific (Occam's Razor Law Is Inapplicable)

The allegation here is that while Occam's Razor Law (i.e. entities are not to be multiplied beyond necessity) may apply to our scientific theories, God is metascientific, that is beyond the realm of Science. So God is not bound to follow the scientific precept of Occam's Razor Law. I think this objection should be rejected for three reasons.

First of all, it should not just be conceded (without overwhelming justification) that any existent thing is beyond the analytical scope of scientific or logical method. It may be true that Science customarily deals with observable or discernible phenomena rather than with unobservable and ultimate phenomena. It may even be true that Science is ill equipped to deal with ultimate phenomena such as God would be. For science there may never be anything that is for long accepted as ultimate, that cannot be questioned and that cannot be rejected in the light of other information or better theories. For instance the atom as the smallest unit of matter is a case in point because ever smaller entities are continually being postulated. Nevertheless there is nothing that exists or may exist that should not be considered in the light of scientific and logical method, the scientific method that includes Occam's Razor Law. After all scientific method is the fount of much technological and all our scientific knowledge, indeed generally of rational knowledge (and irrational 'knowledge' – if such can exist – being irrational has no proper basis).

The second point is that we have no substitute for the scientific or logical method in general and for Occam's Razor Law in particular. If Occam's Razor Law was abandoned there would be no basis of probability nor distinction as between possible rival theories that are judged or arranged to somehow fit the perceived facts, however long, however devious and however fanciful some theories may be. Theories however fanciful or however contrived or however remote they may seem would become indistinguishable in value and credibility from unfanciful, direct and simple theories that just cover the observed phenomena. In that sort of world we would neither attain knowledge nor in practice (if such precepts were really followed) progress far technologically. Such shortcomings could also be awful in theological disputation. God, being omnipotent, could then presumably be said to use his omnipotence to reconcile himself with practically any apparent circumstances. Therefore even the provision about a theory having at least to accommodate itself with observed phenomena would then presumably effectively not apply in the case of an omnipotent God – but if that were the case anything said about God, irrespective of whether God exists would be entirely speculative, incapable of sensible evaluation and probably worthless.

Finally there is in any case no adequate, concrete, methodological reason given why God is so fundamentally different to other hypothetical phenomena that Occam's Razor Law should be abandoned in just his case. Neither its being inconvenient to God nor God (if he exists) being greater than other entities is a valid reason to abandon the principle of Occam's Razor Law.

(vi) This Is No Disproof Of God's Existence

The objection here is that even if, at least in our present state of knowledge, the notion that God exists does not in an explanatory sense conform to Occam's Razor law, that is no proof that God does not exist. In other words just because the existence of God is not the most economical theory available that can explain the situation, it does not mean that God is necessarily non-existent. An analogy might be with a steeple chase horse race. Even though a rank outsider might win the race (as I think happened in the 1967 British Grand National) because all the fancied or form horses fall or get involved in a collision, one would not believe that is likely to happen though it just might happen.

So fanciful or unlikely theories may indeed occasionally prove true but as that is a rare event one would be unwise to believe that that is actually going to be the case. Similarly, if God were to be a possible feature of the Universe, even if God did not appear in a logically likely, economical explanation of the Universe, God might yet indeed exist (as might many other unlikely things). But it would not be logical nor proper to believe from our present state of knowledge that God does exist if he has no explanatory value and so does not very economically fit into the scheme of things. (Of course if for other reasons, God was shown not even to be a possible feature of the Universe, God could not exist and so this discussion would be academic.)

So this objection to the argument is valid in the sense that this argument does not on its own prove that God is an absolutely impossible entity. But this objection is not valid in the sense that this lack of absolute disproof of the existence of God should be an obstacle to our not believing in God. If God is not a probable feature of the Universe, if God does not probably exist, we should not believe in God. In terms of Logic, by which we do live and must live, if God is a postulation that does not have genuine explanatory value for us, it is not an economical postulation and so is not likely to be a correct postulation. So we should not believe in God.

We have now considered in detail possible objections to this argument against the existence of God that God has no explanatory value. It must be conceded that this particular argument is not an absolute disproof of the existence of God. Nevertheless this argument does validly show that according to the principles of Logic and Science the existence of God is not a sensible theory and is therefore not a theory that should be believed in. Absence of real explanatory value (as was pointed out in objection vi) is not an absolute disproof of a phenomenon but it is a valid scientific and logical reason for not believing in a theory. No objection can validly show nor even indicate that postulating God would ultimately have any explanatory value. Nor indeed can any objection show that explanatory value is irrelevant. Therefore none of these objections can undermine this argument that the existence of God should be disbelieved in because the postulation of God is neither warranted by genuine evidence nor is even theoretically credible. So the thrust of this argument is unharmed by any objections that I can foresee.

E. The Argument In Perspective

On the face of it The God Has No Explanatory Value Argument seems to be a strong intellectual argument against the existence of God.

There are points that make this argument formidable. For a start there is no good reason to think God can have genuine explanatory value. For instance it may hypothetically be correct to say that God is in some way self sustaining or it may be correct to say that the Universe is self sustaining. There is no particular reason to think it is God and not the Universe that is self sustaining – and in the absence of such reason there is no sense in postulating God's existence to explain something that can just as readily be explained without God in terms of the Universe itself. Indeed it might even be argued – and I think properly argued – that in these circumstances the postulating of God far from solving the problem is not merely relocating the problem (from the Universe to God) but actually magnifying the problem. In terms of explanation if anything the question of how God (if he exists) came about is an even greater problem than how the Universe came about. This is because God as the creator of the Universe would be even more sophisticated and wondrous than the Universe itself and thus be even harder to explain. Indeed unlike the Universe, God being God through all time could not even have had time to evolve to its present glory. So the postulation of God far from decreasing the problem of explanation can reasonably be said to actually increase the problem of finding an explanation for the existent phenomena.

It might and probably more accurately be said this argument should be termed 'God has negative explanatory value' rather than merely that 'God has no explanatory value' since the notion of God actually increases the explanatory problems it set out to solve. Therefore this argument, strictly speaking, should be that the notion of God should not merely not be believed in but should be positively resisted as it is anti-scientific and anti-logical in its nature. How generous have I been in formulating this argument in more neutral terms!

Furthermore this God has no explanatory value argument against the existence of God is logical enough in its formulation. The first premise, that if he exists God must be the ultimate being and provide the answer to all our ultimate questions, is true within the concept of God, otherwise he would not be God. The second point, that even if God is postulated one can still ask how God came about or what is the purpose of it all, just as one could without postulating God ask how the Universe came about or what is the purpose of it all, is also evidently true. That being the case, the third part of this argument, that postulating God's existence is only unnecessarily adding an extra stage to the argument and has no ultimate explanatory value, follows logically. The fourth part of the argument entails an accurate statement of Occam's Razor Law and then an accurate application of the logic of that law to this case. And the fifth part, the conclusion, that we must therefore not suppose that God exists follows logically and necessarily from the previous stages of this argument.

However this argument is not actually the best argument against the existence of God. Its relative shortcoming is that its conclusion proves only we logically should not believe in God and does not finally prove that God cannot or does not exist. (The other substantial difficulty in practice is in getting people to believe that God is just a postulation and is not an evidenced fact for which all kinds of evidences are cited. This is a major practical difficulty even though all the evidence for God is essentially worthless because it is inadequate to prove God rather than – at most – some powerful daemon exists. Therefore God must in fact be just a theoretical postulation.) Alas there is a difference between an argument that shows (as this argument does) that God is improbable and an argument that effectively proves that God is impossible. True, in both cases we should not believe in God, but this God has no explanatory value argument is not as conclusive as an argument would be that actually shows God's existence is impossible.

So to conclude, The God Has No Explanatory Value Argument is not quite an absolute and final disproof of the existence of God. Yet it is valid as an argument why all rational people living by rational criteria should not actually believe in the existence of God.

CHAPTER 4

The 'This Is Not The Best Possible World' Argument

A. Prologue

If you asked atheists of the present age why they do not believe in God, it is most likely they would claim the evil and suffering that they perceive in the world leads them to suppose that God cannot exist. Atheists in past ages would probably have been of the same opinion. Even most agnostics past and present would have thought the evil apparent within the world a reason for doubting the existence of God.

Clearly the main argument that has traditionally been used to undermine the notion of God is the existence of evil in the world. It is also the main evidence against the existence of God that has been recognised by most philosophers of religion who have believed in the existence of God. Many such people have exercised their minds to attempt to explain away 'the problem of evil'. For instance the two most prominent traditional philosophers of the Christian church, St. Augustine and St. Thomas Aquinas were both concerned to do this.

Of course the ordinary man in the street will readily see evil in natural disasters such as earthquakes and hurricanes and also in crippling diseases and premature deaths (especially in deaths such as cot deaths where the baby never really has an opportunity to enjoy life or exercise his free will).

So even in its traditional formulation the argument against the existence of God because of the evil that exists in the world is a strong argument. While practically nobody denies there is on the face of it a problem of evil to be encountered, many people, including myself, can deny and very credibly deny that any of the explanations offered is a satisfactory answer to the problems raised. For most people the problem of evil is real and visible but generally explanations offered for apparent evil rely on nothing visible in the material world but instead ultimately rely on an element of faith!

Perhaps the most economical formulation of the problem of evil is that used by Charles Bradlaugh (1833-1891), the most prominent British secularist of the nineteenth century. He wrote in his essay A Plea For Atheism – 'Evil is either caused by God or exists independently; but it cannot be caused by God, as in that case he would not be all-good, nor can it exist hostilely, as in that case he would not be all-powerful. If all-good he would desire to annihilate evil, and continued evil contradicts either God's desire or God's ability to prevent it.'

However (as the concern of Augustine and Aquinas implies) such arguments do go back a very long way. Sextus Empiricus in the second century A.D. gave a thorough exposition of the argument in his work Outlines Of Pyrrhonism (Book 3 – Chapter 3) leading to the summary – 'If they say that God controls everything, they make him the author of evil things; if on the other hand, they say that He controls some things only, or that He controls nothing, they are compelled to make God either grudging or impotent, and to do that is quite obviously an impiety.'

As I have already stated, the traditional argument concerning evil and suffering in the world is a strong one. In essence it is:

1. If God exists his qualities necessarily include being all-good and all-powerful (and indeed in traditional belief creating the world).

2. Evil is the antithesis of good and of God's goodness.

3. But we observe that evil, the antithesis of Good, occurs in this (God's) world.

4. Therefore God was either not able to prevent evil through not being all-powerful or not willing to prevent evil through not being all-good. In both eventualities it cannot be that God (as formulated in 1 above) exists.

It is noteworthy that all the major efforts to undermine or defeat this argument against the existence of God based on evil in this world have been directed at the third of the four statements above.

Nobody of importance denies that God is essentially both all-good and all-powerful (although some such as Aquinas qualify that by saying God cannot do the logically impossible such as create a square circle but that is irrelevant here).

Furthermore nobody denies that evil is the antithesis of Good and of a supposed God's goodness. Nobody of significance even denies that if any real evil exists in the world without proper reason it is indeed evidence that God does not exist.

All the real effort is concerned at undermining the third point, that we observe evil occurs in the world. Even then nobody really denies that apparent evil exists in the world. The usual argument is essentially that we cannot live in an apparently perfect world but we do live in as good a world as is feasible. The usual explanation is that God gave us freewill which is the most perfect of gifts but because of the nature of freewill and of our own selves, we cannot have both freewill and apparent perfection – and freewill is claimed to be the greater good than apparent perfection. So it is this third premise (that we observe real evil) in this argument that needs to be strengthened in the face of counter-attacks (admittedly of the indirect sort that apparent evil is not real evil) from monotheists.

So I am going to reformulate the basic argument from evil against God's existence into a new and even stronger argument. However it is well worth noting that theologians' defences to the traditional argument are really no more than insubstantial camouflage that confuses people. Theologians claim that though the world includes apparent elements of evil, we can reasonably have faith that our existence is in reality permeated by God's love and is not ultimately engulfed by genuine evil. But, as Bertrand Russell (1872-1970) has pointed out (in Why I Am Not A Christian) it is neither a natural nor a sensible assumption to suppose that a thing which is defective on the surface is any better underneath the surface.

Furthermore the famous Prussian philosopher Gottfried Wilhelm Leibniz (1646-1716), although he was a convinced theist argued that to be the product of God and God's creation this world must be the best possible world. No other type of world can be compatible with 'the glory of God'. Leibniz wrote, 'Neither am I able to approve of the opinion of certain modern writers who boldly maintain that that which God has made is not perfect in the highest degree, and that he might have done better. It seems to me that the consequences of such an opinion are wholly inconsistent with the glory of God... I think that one acts imperfectly if he acts with less perfection than he is capable of.' – Discourse On Metaphysics, Section III. Leibniz famously proceeded to argue that though this world might seem imperfect it is actually the best possible world. Leibniz is considered to be authoritative in many matters. Nevertheless he is not it seems supported by other major philosophers in his absolute and logically correct insistence that if God exists the only world he (being supremely good and supremely powerful) could have created is the best possible world. Nor is he supported in his assertions that defy all credibility that this world is actually in every way the best possible world which even omnipotent power could have created! Yet at least Leibniz attempted to argue logically in this matter whereas other theists have failed to adhere to proper logical argumentation in the vexed question of the supposed coexistence of God with imperfections in this world.

At this point it is worth noting, especially as it is not generally known, that George Grote (1794-1871), a leading British scholar of ancient Greek history, in a private letter went some of the way informally in my direction towards reformulating the argument from evil against God's existence. He wrote, 'where there is a grain of misery existing – a single grain – this must be because the Maker of it (granting the hypothesis) either wants the will or wants the power to prevent it. The evil that exists is a plain proof that there is no being (i.e. God) existing... an aching finger proves that there can be none such.' – G GROTE (Letter c1824 – A2.14.2 – as printed in Chapter 9, Section I of a book entitled 'A History Of Atheism In Britain From Hobbes To Russell' by David Berman). This is a better formulation of the argument from evil because it argues that the amount of genuine evil that needs to exist to disprove God's existence need only be slight or minimal. Yet Grote has not quite absolutely proved that an aching finger is unnecessary and unwarranted and so is not a necessary evil. He took that as obvious but I fear that theologians would still try to argue, however implausibly, that every aching finger is indeed necessary to the divine scheme of things!

In attempting to reformulate the basic atheistic argument in yet stronger terms I am not denying that the argument as traditionally formulated is already a strong argument! Nevertheless I am going to propose a new argument that is substantially a reformulation of this argument against God because of the evil in this world so as to permit theists even less scope to confuse the issue. My innovative insight is to assert that to exist God must be not just good but supremely good. God must be the best possible entity, otherwise he would not be God. For instance there couldn't be a situation where some people, though imperfect, are morally better than God. Consequently in all logic this allegedly God-created world must not just have an absence of evil but must be the best possible world if God really created it. God being supremely good (not merely good), the best possible entity, is therefore bound to create not merely a good world but the best possible world, thus giving its inhabitants the best possible arrangements within which to live. Therefore if it is found that we do not live in what is hypothetically the best of all possible worlds, our world is not then the product of a supremely good creator and therefore God did not ultimately create the world – and therefore God does not exist. So if we can prove that we do not live in the best of all possible worlds we can therefore prove that God does not exist. Therefore to disprove God's existence we need only prove that the Universe (or any part of the Universe) is not the best possible Universe. My second and supplementary insight is that the imperfection of the world (and therefore of the Universe) can be proved by the sheer inconsistency within the world that is gratuitous and is unrelated either to morality or to functional necessity.

I suggest the following as a detailed version of my own argument:

a) If God exists his qualities include being eternal, supremely good and supremely powerful and being ultimately the creator (and sustainer) of the world.

b) Therefore God (being supremely good and supremely powerful) must have created the best possible world if he exists.

c) Living conditions in the world are now radically different to what they were 500 years ago.

d) Therefore living conditions now or living conditions in the world 500 years ago cannot constitute the best possible world in terms of its living conditions. (Either it is the best possible thing to live in the modern, technologically developed world or otherwise to live in a primitive world or neither but not both.)

e) Therefore 'God' has not created the best possible world either 500 years ago or now or at neither time. (Note: Technological development is not a matter of moral worth, still less of pre-birth moral worth, but either of collective brainpower or God's will.)

f) Therefore taking the world as a whole scheme over time 'God' has not created the best possible world.

g) Therefore the undeniable evidence of this world contradicts the existence of a God whose qualities are as cited in the premises (i.e. a God that is both all-powerful and all-good).

h) So God cannot be our creator, supremely good and supremely powerful though he must have all those qualities to exist as God.

i) Therefore God cannot exist.

The crux of this argument is that instead of setting out to prove that there is real (as well as apparent) evil in the world, I have reduced what has to be proved to that we do not live in the best possible world when everything is taken into account.

B. Summary Of The Argument

1. God if he exists must be omnipotent, supremely good and our ultimate creator.

2. Therefore an existent God (being supremely good and competent) would have created the best possible world (if he created anything).

3. As the world is inconsistent (between ages and people) it cannot all be the best possible world.

4. Therefore as the world is not the best possible world, God cannot exist.

C. Explaining The Argument

The first premise of the argument that God must be omnipotent (or at any rate 'maximally powerful' in terms of Logic), supremely good and our ultimate creator is simply definitional. God would not exist as a monotheistic God if he lacked omnipotence or supreme goodness or was not ultimately our creator. So there can be no dispute about any of those qualities (i.e. omnipotence, supreme goodness and ultimate creation) if it is God we are talking about.

The point that follows, that as a consequence of God's qualities God must have created the best possible world if he created any world at all is a point that follows entirely logically from God's stated qualities. The point is that God cannot be merely good but must be supremely good or all-good. God must be good right through, supremely good not just some of the time but all the time. Otherwise one could say that though we have a good God, we do not have the best possible, the best conceivable God. In other words we would have a 'God' who is somewhat soiled or somewhat flawed. Even though 'God' had it in his power (in his omnipotence) to act better and create a better world and be all-good he deliberately opted not to. So being thus deficient in character (or goodness) he would not in reality be a perfectly good example to the world. After all some humans might choose, if given the advantage of omnipotence to be supremely good, and so potentially at least they would be better in character than God! So for God not to create absolutely the best possible world which omnipotence can create would be an imperfection in God's character which is not compatible with being a supremely good God. So God if he exists must have created and sustained not merely a predominantly good world but the very best, most flawless possible world.

The next point is to establish that we do not live in the best possible world (or alternatively that there is genuine evil in the world). Conventionally this is just assumed upon empirical observation by most anti-theists. However an assumption, even a common assumption, does not quite constitute proof. So I suggest some proof should be found for this assumption. One can of course say that religions, religious Scriptures, alleged statements from God, and religious people all (or almost all) themselves accept that there is at least sometimes some evil in the world. All the political priests who believe in political action to improve the world and even those who believe in good works and helping charities to improve the world obviously do not believe we live in the best possible world. Nor evidently did Christ believe that the world was perfect when he encouraged people to behave in the manner of the Good Samaritan and not like others who just passed by oblivious to human suffering (Luke 10. 30-37). Even more strikingly the Biblical 'God' himself declared that he had not made a perfect world. In Genesis – 'God said, "This race of men whom I have created, I will wipe off the face of the Earth – man and beast, reptiles and birds, I am sorry that I ever made them".' (Genesis 6.7). Far from making the best of a bad job God would kill off his mistakes by flood which I suspect isn't a pleasant death! However in case anybody should think contrary to 'God's' own reported words in Genesis that God has created the best possible world I suggest that the best logical approach for finding some defect in the world is to examine the inconsistency of the world. It is then not necessary to determine which version is perfect and which is imperfect. One can merely say that as some things differ incompatibly with each other, things cannot all be perfect. For instance some people are born blind and some people are born sighted. Although we might naturally think it is better to be born sighted, even if we are wrong (and it is better to be born blind) it can scarcely be perfect for some people to be by nature sighted and some to be by nature blind. Another instance concerns human technological development. In respect of technological development we all live in a quite technologically advanced world and even the remotest regions in the world are beginning to be affected by advanced technology. And there certainly was a lack of advanced technology in the past. So there is here a fundamental inconsistency between ages in the human condition. As there was very little or no technological change for many thousands of years it cannot reasonably be claimed that it is necessary for the level of available technology to differ drastically and fundamentally between ages. Nor can it intelligently be claimed that the technological environment into which people are born is determined or predetermined by the exercise of their own individual freewill for which they are morally and personally responsible. Yet it cannot possibly be that making the human environment (which is fundamental to human life) primitive in its technological capacity in some ages and advanced in its technological capacity in other ages constitutes the best possible world in all ages. While neither our relatively advanced technological ability nor the previous relatively primitive technological ability may be the form which the best possible world would take, they cannot both be elements of the best possible world. Therefore if 'God' created and sustained the world both in the past and in the present as he must have done to be God, he has not at all times provided the best possible world.

In conclusion, God, being by definition supremely good and omnipotent and our creator, would if he existed have created the best possible world. Yet we can be sure (either because of 'God's' alleged statements in religion or because of the fundamental yet unnecessary inconsistency in the world) that the world taken as a whole throughout the ages is not the best possible world. Therefore it is logically shown that God cannot actually exist. Therefore as God cannot exist within the parameters of Logic, God cannot and does not exist at all.

D. Possible Objections To The Argument

I shall now consider various possible objections to this argument against the existence of God based upon this not being the best possible world and therefore as such not being compatible with the existence of God.

(i) God Need Not Create The Best Possible World

This argument seeks to show that God since he must be the most supremely good conceivable entity is logically bound to create the best possible world. I can see no logical way to challenge the definition of God as including (so far as Logic permits) omnipotence and supreme goodness or the corollary that he is bound in those circumstances to create the best possible world. Yet it must be admitted that most theologians do not think of this as the best possible world and still believe in God's existence. Indeed Leibniz (1646-1716) has been widely reviled for suggesting we live in the best possible world. In fact many religious doctrines such as the perfection to be found in an afterlife in Heaven rather than on Earth, or such as the Fall of Man from near perfection in the Garden of Eden or such as the Second Coming of Jesus Christ affirm this view that our world is presently imperfect. One often held view (at least so far as natural disasters are concerned) is that we do not live in the best possible world as yet but at least we live in a world which is progressing on the way to being the best possible world.

However I can see no logical foundation for the view that an imperfect world (even a temporarily imperfect world developing into perfection) is compatible with God's existence. Nor can I see that imperfection now for which those now alive suffer even has any significant improving effect upon people in the future. I doubt the notion that people are much influenced by knowledge of historical development which in turn justifies that historical development. The fact of the matter is that human historical experience is for the most part lost or distorted and that very few people are much interested in History. Even fewer people have an accurate appreciation of History and practically nobody acts in their everyday lives perpetually in the conscious light of previous human history. However even more fundamental is the fact that supreme goodness and indeed the best possible world are not notions that God can legitimately build up over time. God being supremely good and omnipotent must produce the best possible world all the time. Surely it is better and therefore essential to supreme goodness to be perfect all the time and everywhere rather than just to be perfect (after much imperfection) towards the end of time? For instance no chocolate factory owner would escape immediate enforcement of health and safety regulations by claiming that his chocolates are downright unsafe now and for the foreseeable future but they will eventually improve and ultimately reach perfection (and therefore he is indeed a supremely good chocolate manufacturer!) – his chocolates are expected to be good at all times. So why should not God (who must be supremely good if he exists) be held to being supremely good and creating perfection all the time rather than just for some of the time?

I suppose the view might also be theoretically put (for such a view can scarcely be based upon practical observation of this world) that a world that is less than perfect need not necessarily be evil. One can have the greatest pleasure or one can have great pleasure or indeed merely pleasure – and pleasure even in a merely slight degree is not pain. However that view is not applicable to perfection where anything short of perfection must to some degree be imperfection. Furthermore and more fundamentally, God is not a man (who might be good or very good) but is supremely good and therefore only the best, only the very best possible arrangement is in accordance with the combination of his supreme goodness and his supreme power!

So it is indeed convenient for theists to account for any imperfections in this world by claiming that God need not create nor sustain the best possible world but that view is not logically sustainable.

(ii) This Is The Best Possible World

It may be suggested that this is the best possible world, although that is a view which seems contradictory to empirical evidence and even contrary to religious Scriptures and is held by very few people. However where this view is held or suggested it is usually supposed that human freewill is such an overwhelmingly good thing that it outweighs all the other great evils which apparently exist and which freewill is claimed to cause. Yet in practice people do not for instance allow freewill to extend even to driving without a seatbelt, let alone to their children running into danger in front of moving cars on the roads even if that is momentarily an act of their freewill. As even humans do not see freewill as an excuse for running dangerous risks, why should God excuse all kinds of evils with human freewill? Yet even freewill does not really account for natural disasters and naturally caused suffering and for the suffering of babies who may die before they even attain genuine freewill. Furthermore it seems freewill is a very strange phenomenon. Freewill is clearly bridled in many ways – we are not free to live yet cease from eating, breathing, sleeping or abiding by the irksome physical limitations of our bodies. Yet freewill is apparently unbridled according to theologians in its freedom to cause great evil (though seemingly some people who command followers or money or advanced technology have even greater freedom to cause evil than others!).

So surely it cannot be supposed that this is the best possible world even divine omnipotence can conceivably create. It would be absurd to suppose that improving this world (even other than by the personal human effort which most religions and clergy call for) is a logical impossibility and contradiction in terms even in respect of divine omnipotence. Who would believe that improving our world in any way is an impossibility in the same way as changing the past, producing a square circle or inventing a greater God are supposedly logical contradictions in terms even for God? Furthermore we know that the idea that this is the best possible world is not merely absurd but also illogical. As we know different types of physical conditions (some of which are presumably better and some harsher or worse) have existed in our world at different times or even at the same time for different people, so we logically know that over time this cannot always have been the best possible world. Therefore this objection is not merely apparently absurd but also plain wrong.

(iii) We Cannot Prove This Is Not The Best Possible World

According to this objection the attempted proof (by inconsistency or even by allegedly divine statements) that our world is not the best possible world is not sufficient to logically prove the point.

Some, particularly Easterners, might claim that all evil is an illusion (Eastern 'maya') but even if that were so in one sense, the illusion is itself an evil and a cause of imperfection.

Another suggestion some may make is that apparent inconsistencies in our physical environment and other circumstances can be explained. One need only recognise that because people (and animals) are all different in temperament and character the best possible world is properly constituted by putting different people into different ages and into different circumstances. That is somewhat implausible because we humans are not all that different from each other and all can suffer in many similar ways (e.g. fires, earthquakes etc). Nor does that explain why so much apparently unjust suffering (e.g. childhood leukaemia) and so many apparently unnecessary problems (e.g. indiscriminate natural disasters) occur in the world.

Another ploy could be to suggest that for all we know even if this world is seemingly imperfect every other possible alternative scenario would actually be worse – and so this world is the very best that even divine omnipotence can actually manage. However it is ridiculous to claim that it is beyond the power of even omnipotence merely to improve somewhat at least some things. Surely one could make some experiences, even death (if death there must be), in some instances unpainful or at least less painful instead of extremely painful.

So we can leave anybody who wants to argue that this is the best possible world floundering in absurdity, such as having to say that even small differences in temperament between different people justify terribly different and often very 'deprived' circumstances. Furthermore according to such a claim this is the best possible world even an omnipotent God (despite what we and indeed most religious people and religious scriptures suppose) could possibly have created. Supposedly God could not have created and sustained a better world even to the extent of allowing the best technology for humans to exist at all times instead of only at certain times! So to claim this is the best of all possible worlds is to contradict all the empirical evidence available to us and to disown the attitude of every major monotheistic religion, and presumably therefore to disown every major religion! Indeed because of the actual hardships people suffer no religion that claims we live in the best possible world would ever have been credible or survived! In fact far from asserting that people don't suffer on Earth, religions have tended to gain their adherents by offering a means, albeit a fallacious means, to enable people to find an eventual way out of suffering, if not in this life then in the next life, by following them and prayer or meditation.

So even if the proof through inconsistency that this is not the best possible world were inadequate (which it is not), it just isn't credible in the real world to believe this is the best possible world!

(iv) The Imperfection Of This World Is In The Context Of An Everlasting Afterlife

The objection here is that if there is suffering in our brief lives in this world, this should be seen within the context of an eternal afterlife for which some suffering here is necessary to determine our fate in the afterlife. In any case any injustices here on Earth will be redeemed in the afterlife. Our world is a kind of necessary examination paper for entry into an afterlife of either an eternal paradise in Heaven or eternal punishment in Hell.

This is a very traditional populist explanation for any evils that might arise in this world. It has been preached by many priests and believed in by many people over the centuries. Admittedly it has not been quite so popular among the leading theologians which is unsurprising as it is intellectually riddled with difficulties in many respects. This notion is also less commonly believed in today but is still quite widely believed in by the general public and some religiously fundamentalist priests and mullahs.

The first and obvious point to make is that the suffering on Earth is real but Heaven and Hell are only hypothetical and may well not exist. Indeed I say any sensible or rational person would at least doubt, if not entirely dismiss, the existence of an afterlife, let alone the doctrine of an afterlife characterised by essentially only two extreme habitats, Heaven and Hell! Even many modern bishops now disbelieve in at least part of this doctrine and think Hell (if not, as some of the most liberal of their number now think, Heaven as well) just does not exist. The non-existence of even Hell (let alone the non-existence of Heaven) certainly undermines the whole doctrine that suffering on Earth is necessary to determine by our actions our fate in the afterlife.

However even if one were theoretically to suppose there might be an afterlife wherein our fate is determined by our behaviour on this Earth (which is in itself a logical non-sequitur even if there was an afterlife), some disturbing problems remain. For a start is it really necessary for a supposedly omniscient God, even if despite his omnipotence he somehow chose to create very imperfect humans in the first place to put his creatures through torment and suffering just to decide their future destination? After all a good motor mechanic would not need to take a car through a bumpy test run to see whether it would be roadworthy or not. If sufficiently skilled he might be able to see that just by examining it and even if he needed to take it on a test run, he would know enough from taking it on smooth tarmaced roads rather than through tracks full of potholes. A run along smooth roads would be sufficient for him to discover any faults which would make it unroadworthy. This is done without omnipotence, just a modicum of skill. Is God really less skilled that a good motor mechanic? So even if this life were an examination with a view to the future, there is no need for such great imperfection (rather than a small amount of imperfection) and suffering on Earth to test for their future the worthiness of people or 'souls'. A little bit of hardship or imperfection rather than extensive imperfection or hardship would surely do. Anyhow hardship and suffering comes disproportionately to some rather than to others. Indeed infants who never attain much consciousness and die suddenly from say cot death are never meaningfully tested at all! So even if suffering was hypothetically necessary, the suffering and imperfections on Earth are clearly excessive for it to have derived from an omnipotent, omniscient creator who is supremely good, that is from a monotheistic God!

Furthermore the concept of Hell for supposedly failing the test of life on Earth also has problems, especially in the context of modern human thought. An eternal punishment for a small period on Earth of imperfection or even disobedience to God, indeed a God that does not even clearly or manifestly exist, is surely disproportionate and unfair. Surely Hell now comes within the modern understanding of torture or cruel and unusual punishment which is now forbidden in most civilised countries even for imperfect people, let alone for a supremely good God to inflict. Furthermore if the idea is to encourage people to behave or learn properly, as is the idea of education in schools, a good teacher, be he human or presumably God, is able to prevail upon those in his care to behave well and learn diligently and thus pass their examinations. If even a good teacher can coax pupils into success, why does God fail and just consign his God-made rejects into Hell?

Then there is the more fundamental problem that even if there is a perfect afterlife, time spent on Earth is still part of a person's (or soul's) life experience and must count as an imperfection within that life experience. Even if existence on this Earth were only a small part of one's whole existence, its imperfections and suffering means that one's existence as a whole and indeed the whole system cannot be perfect. At best it is like having a good holiday that gets off to a thoroughly bad start. It is like a holidaymaker who is delayed for several miserable hours at the airport and has an outward flight where the turbulence causes his hot drinks to spill all over him but then finds the hotel at the other end is very good indeed. One would not say that the holiday experience was perfect nor that it could not be improved upon, even if in the end it was not too bad overall. One would say the holiday could have been better and certainly the organisers, be it humans or God, should have done better – indeed it had such imperfections that it could not have been provided by an entirely perfect entity. Likewise suppose a restaurant had a large kitchen which was mostly immaculately clean but at one corner there was a mess, an accumulation of verminous rubbish. Then far from public health officials who inspected it saying it was perfect, or even satisfactory, they would probably prosecute the restaurant owner for the shortcomings in that little corner. Likewise if in the whole Universe or whole of our lives (or existences) there is an imperfect or defective small portion (our lives on Earth), the entire Universe is somewhat imperfect and cannot be under the control or supervision of a perfect God.

So this notion that an imperfect Earth can be redeemed by an afterlife and discounted as a portion (even if merely hypothetically it is not the whole) of our lives (or existences) is wrong. However (relatively) short the time we spend on Earth suffering or losing out within an imperfect world, that is still part of the Universe and must make the Universe as a whole somewhat imperfect. Just as lost time can never be redeemed nor recovered, imperfection which we suffer can never be redeemed nor fully recovered even should (which is unlikely) we live (or exist) from hereon unto eternity. An imperfect Earth is a contamination of some (or all) of our real time that cannot in Logic (nor of course in reality) be a part of the best possible Universe – it proves that we do not live in the best possible world, nor indeed in a system created by a monotheistic and perfect God!

(v) Variety Is Necessary

The possible objection here is that variety is so overwhelmingly necessary to the world that it is worth (indeed entails) a certain amount of apparent imperfection (in the same way that some theists think that freewill is worth a price in imperfection). Indeed it can be argued that there is a paradox about the very concept of the best possible world. If one constructs the best possible state of affairs such a scenario would be static because all the changes from it, the best, must be for the worse. Yet a static, undynamic, unchanging state of affairs cannot be the best possible state of affairs because it lacks variety. So there is perhaps a paradox here. Variety necessarily entails imperfection ('various' arrangements cannot all be the best possible arrangement of the Universe) – yet absence of variety is also itself an imperfection because it lacks dynamism and therefore removes much interest from life.

I confess I would not know quite how to resolve the paradox of imperfection through variety and imperfection without variety but I do know that in the Universe in which we live that is clearly an academic question! Our Universe is so far short of perfection that the imperfection of our world cannot properly be accounted for merely by the possible need for variety. One might reasonably argue that a small amount of apparent imperfection may be needed in the Universe to keep it varied, dynamic and changing and so make it properly challenging and interesting. However one cannot reasonably nor sensibly claim so much apparently gratuitous trouble and suffering is necessitated merely by the requirement to keep the Universe interesting rather than static and boring. So one might argue the need for a sometimes less than maximally pleasurable state of affairs but one cannot merely for this reason (variety) properly argue a need for a frequently painful and often unfairly painful Universe. One can hardly argue that the best possible world merely because of the hypothetical need for some variety entailed the need for illnesses (such as leprosy) that cause much suffering which often in any case later generations are able to cure and in fact live without! If life is more pleasurable and entails much less suffering in some ages than in other ages with the scope for variety still maintained in all ages, we cannot validly argue that such (excessive) suffering is necessary for either variety or for maintaining one's interest in the Universe. So one cannot therefore argue that historically (or even geographically) speaking our world can be the best of all possible worlds even given the possible need for a certain amount of variety.

So though a possible need for variety in life might conceivably justify just a small element of apparent imperfection, it cannot justify anywhere near the amount of imperfection that actually exists in our world. Therefore even granting the possible importance of variety and making allowance for that we cannot be said to live in the best possible world or even in anything anywhere approaching the best possible world.

(vi) There Is No Such Thing As The Best Possible World

It is I think possible to argue that talk of living in the best possible world is nonsensical because there is no such thing as 'good' or 'bad' and therefore there is no such thing as 'best possible'. There is no objective standard nor graduation nor measure of things out in the sky or anywhere else from which 'good' and 'best' can properly be derived. Even though pain and joy evidently exist in an empirical sense, it can also be said that there is no absolute standard of good and bad to correlate with them. It would be taking such considerations very far to divorce the concept of joy and pain from a supremely loving and personal God (and God is supposedly in Christianity at least both loving and personal) but I am myself inclined to agree there is no absolute impersonal standard of good and bad.

However if one – perhaps correctly – eliminates goodness and thus supreme goodness from the definition of God, one must also take the consequences of doing that. So if there is no absolute standard of good and bad, God cannot then be a morally worthy entity because God cannot then point to standards of goodness since they ultimately do not exist and so are existentially meaningless. In that case God cannot legitimately be worshipped as a moral example, since there is ultimately no morality of good or bad to be an example for.

If God should not be worshipped and cannot ultimately be looked to on account of ethical inspiration, God (if he exists in other respects) is no more than a powerful daemon – he might be bowed to on account of his power but he cannot worthily be worshipped in a religious manner. Such an entity not only should not be worshipped as religiously worthy but also may not in the absence of supreme goodness even be considered to be God. This is because he would then lack an essential quality of God, namely supreme goodness (even though the absence of supreme goodness is enforced through the meaninglessness or absence of any absolute scale of goodness).

So I concede it may be that there is in an absolute sense no such thing as a 'best possible' world though it is more difficult to argue that there is no such thing even for an omnipotent being as a 'most lovingly or most humanely constructed world'. Yet if that is the case then in the absence of 'supreme goodness' there can presumably definitionally be no God. Certainly in the absence of an example of 'supreme goodness' there can be no legitimate God-based religion nor legitimate worship of God (since people might legitimately worship an entity of supreme goodness but not merely naked power).

(vii) God's Ways Are Mysterious And Unfathomable

When theists are in a bind, they often resort to the response that God moves in mysterious ways which are unfathomable to us and though they feel sure that God exists they don't know all the ways in which God operates. So in this case they may assert that they do not know the answer to the apparent logic of this argument but they are sure that God exists in a way which we can know little of.

The problem with this attempt to cloud and mystify the issue is that the logic involved in this particular argument is really very straightforward and fathomable. There is no proper scope for anything that is relevant yet unfathomable. It is simply definitional to state that God if he exists must be omnipotent, supremely good and our ultimate creator – otherwise he would not be God. It is pure logic that as a consequence of his supreme goodness and power to do so God (if he exists) must have created the best possible world – there is no logical alternative to that which would still maintain 'God' as God. There is nothing difficult in finding some inconsistencies in our world (or indeed religious statements and some allegedly God-uttered statements) which show that our world is not in all respects and at all times the best possible world. Indeed this point has nothing directly to do with God – it comes from our standpoint and observation combined with some logic. Therefore as the world is not the best possible world it cannot in the premises ultimately be God's creation. That follows logically. Nor can the world have been created in defiance of an omnipotent God. Therefore God does not exist. This argument is nowhere concerned with the ways in which God operates (mysteriously or otherwise!). This argument is only concerned with analysing some qualities that would be essential for God and showing that at least in some respects our world is not compatible with being a product of those (i.e. God's) necessary qualities.

So mystery is irrelevant to this argument and there is really nothing difficult to be fathomed. Some of God's indisputable essential qualities (omnipotence, ultimate creator and supreme goodness) are here identified. Then the world is shown by simple observation of the world (not of God!) not to be consistent in key respects with God's possible existence. That being the case as the world certainly exists, God is shown not to exist. So I cannot see any validity to this particular objection.

So in relation to all these possible objections, the only substantive point that causes some trouble is that there is doubt over whether 'good' and 'bad' have any objective rather than merely human subjective meaning. However even there if good and evil do not actually exist in ultimate terms, there are two possible ways to proceed, neither of which rescues monotheism. Either one may resort to an alternative stipulation that God is maximally 'humane' or 'loving' and replace the notion of 'the best possible world' with 'the most humanely or most lovingly constructed world' in which case everything proceeds as before. Or one gives up the notion of any absolute morality in which case 'God' necessarily cannot have a moral dimension and so is no longer in reality God and he is no more than a very powerful daemon and is certainly not worthy of religious worship.

E. The Argument In Perspective

This argument against the existence of God is in essence (like the traditional argument of suffering in the world) an argument that our world as we observe it and indeed as it exists is necessarily incompatible with the existence of God. Unlike other arguments in this book this argument is not so much about the logical difficulties inherent within God's essential qualities but about the incompatibility of God's existence with the world we live in and observe. The point of this argument is to show that our world is so bad that it is incompatible with the existence of an entity that is supremely good and supremely powerful that created and sustains it, as God definitionally must be. The force of this argument is that God being supremely good and supremely powerful must necessarily be good right through, everywhere. So God must make and keep good the whole of the Universe, not just parts of the Universe. Furthermore, God being supremely good, the Universe God created must not just be a somewhat good or on-balance good Universe but must necessarily be the best possible Universe. Therefore if the Universe even in merely some of its parts including even small parts like our Earth is not the best possible Universe, it is not compatible with the existence of God. This argument seeks to prove first that our world must (as demonstrated above) be the best possible world if it is to be compatible with the existence of God and secondly that our world is in actual fact not the best possible world and so is not compatible with the existence of God. Moreover in such circumstances since the Universe undoubtedly does exist, God cannot exist.

The first premise of this argument (i.e. God if he exists must be omnipotent, supremely good and our ultimate creator) is definitional and correct since if it was not true the entity featured could not be God. The conclusion (i.e. that God cannot exist) also follows entirely logically if the other three parts of the argument are correct. This only leaves the two middle propositions which are the innovative parts of this argument.

I cannot see how we can logically escape from the proposition that a supremely good (indeed morally perfect) and omnipotent God would have created not merely a good but the best possible world. If there is any doubt about that proposition it exists in the notion that there is objectively speaking such a thing as 'good' or 'bad' and therefore such a thing as 'best possible'. However if there is no such thing as 'good' or 'supreme goodness' in objective terms, then in the absence of a moral dimension God cannot exist as God because nothing more than a powerful daemon can then conceivably or definitionally exist. So we can state on this point that if God exists he is supremely good (or at least supremely benevolent) and omnipotent and so he must inevitably have created the best possible world.

We come now to the third point, that a deficiency in terms of our world being the best possible world can be detected by the fundamental inconsistencies we can see in the world. Certainly if there really are such inconsistencies this argument is valid and on the face of it there clearly are such inconsistencies. Few would say otherwise. However somebody might claim that all people – indeed all creatures – are fundamentally different and therefore very different conditions are appropriate in terms of being the best possible conditions in respect of different people. Obviously the atheist could reply firstly that people are not all that different to justify so much difference in living conditions and secondly we can all think of (and often achieve by hard work or good luck or the help of others) changes in our own conditions which would improve matters. Indeed even religious scriptures and religious doctrines, let alone common opinion and common sense, all confirm that we do not live in the best possible world.

So this argument reduces the notion of God to a logical absurdity, the absurdity being either that God is compatible with anything other than the best possible world or that this world is the best possible world. This argument that this is not the best possible world is far superior to the usual argument against the existence of God deriving from some elements of evil existing in the world. This argument invalidates many attempted theistic defences (such as the alleged mere preponderance of good over evil) to the existence of evil in the world. It also disproves the general religious notion, as indeed expressed in the Bible, that God exists yet the world is imperfect (and can be improved though not perfected by our own actions).

In conclusion I assert that this argument against God's existence deriving from this not being the best possible world is a logical disproof of conventional religion. It also reduces the notion of a monotheistic God to thorough absurdity. This is because it is logically necessary to believe this is the best possible world for the world to be compatible with the existence of a supremely good and omnipotent God (i.e. a monotheistic God) and yet it is absurd to believe this world always has been and is comprehensively the best possible world. So it is completely absurd and irrational to believe in the existence of God. Therefore this argument does prove that we should not believe in the existence of God. With God needing to be what it must be to exist as God and the world being what it is, the two, the concept of God and our world are logically mutually incompatible. Since we can be sure that our world exists (even if we are sometimes deluded – yet another imperfection in the world! – about it) we can therefore be absolutely sure that God does not exist.

CHAPTER 5

The Universal Uncertainty Argument

A. Prologue

This is my favourite argument against the existence of God and I believe it is a decisive and absolute disproof of the existence of God. It also approaches the matter from a novel angle, concentrating on the problems facing a potential (or 'candidate') God rather than primarily looking at things from the human perspective, as most other arguments do. I shall therefore elaborate this argument even more thoroughly than I have done with the other arguments and consequently I am devoting more space to it.

So far as I know (and I have looked carefully into this), this Universal Uncertainty Argument against the existence of God is essentially original to me. Yet I acknowledge that unbeknown to me when I thought of and drafted this argument, Roland Puccetti (1924-1995) had actually stated in abbreviated form a somewhat similar (at least in outline) argument to mine. It was printed in the Australasian Journal of Philosophy 41 (1963) 92-93 and reprinted in the book The Impossibility Of God, edited by Martin and Monnier. Puccetti said in his argument that since God cannot know the totality of facts constituting the Universe, God cannot be omniscient and so God (who must necessarily be omniscient) cannot exist. Unfortunately a premise and method of arguing Puccetti used to show that God cannot be omniscient seems to be that in order to be omniscient an entity must be able to think what is unthinkable which is impossible. He says he derived this notion from Ludwig Wittgenstein (1889-1951). However that reasoning may well be and even seems to me to be fallacious. In any case so far as I know Puccetti's argumentation is not as comprehensive as mine and does not deal explicitly with the vital issues I draw attention to of the impossibility of the identification and indeed self-identification of God. Nevertheless Puccetti's argument is of some interest, as indeed are other anti-theological arguments he used elsewhere in his writings.

The philosophy of religion is not a new subject and arguments about the existence or even non-existence of God go back thousands of years at the very least.

So I am doing nothing unusual in arguing about the possible existence of God. However where I am doing something unusual is in not using the traditional orthodox approach to discussing the existence of God. I am using a very different unorthodox approach that is practically the opposite to the orthodox, generally used approach in at least four significant ways. I think the novel result I have come up with has a lot to do with the novel approach I have adopted in this argument. So let me point out in an exact way the four major differences between my unorthodox approach here and the orthodox way of looking at things.

In the first place nowadays the very attempt to actually prove or disprove the existence of God is unorthodox. People, especially philosophers, in the twentieth century have generally given up the attempt to reach any proof or disproof of God's existence as completely doomed. Some twentieth century philosophers like the logical positivists (such as Alfred Ayer), having despaired of proving or disproving the existence of God, then disputed whether the very question of the existence or non-existence of God is even a meaningful question. I trust that in defining 'the God concept' in terms of God's necessary qualities I am thereby showing that the concept at any rate of God is distinct and meaningful. The more common and less esoteric modern view is that 'I cannot prove God exists and you cannot prove God does not exist, so belief in God is absolutely and inevitably a matter of faith.' That is the common view, along with its implied and despairing corollary that it is not even worth looking at supposed proofs and disproofs of the existence of God because none of them can possibly succeed anyhow. So modern views tend to be so cynical and so pessimistic about the possibility of proving or disproving God's existence that few people are prepared to look seriously into the matter to begin with. Interestingly this was not always the case nor even the case for most of Western history right up until at least the nineteenth century. Many of the great philosophers such as Plato, Aristotle, Aquinas, Descartes and Leibniz were very ready to believe that the existence of God could be intellectually proved. Sundry other prominent thinkers such as Anselm, Bishop Berkeley and even Immanuel Kant put forward new and, as they supposed, definitive proofs of the existence of God. The general – and I think correct – consensus of opinion is that all these attempts of even these great thinkers to actually prove the existence of God are logically flawed and therefore invalid. Perhaps because of these failures of even the most eminent philosophers the mood has become one of not merely giving up trying to discover a proof or disproof of God's existence but even of believing that no such proof or disproof can ever be theoretically possible. This despair may be understandable but this belief in failure can become self fulfilling. After all if almost nobody is going to seriously try to find a proof, of course it is overwhelmingly likely that no proof will then be forthcoming! So my first break with the modern conventional approach to the question of the existence of God is to believe that the question of the existence of God may actually be capable of absolute proof or disproof. That belief is important just to attempt to prove or disprove the existence of God in the first place.

My second break with the conventional approach is to attempt not an absolute proof but an absolute disproof of the existence of an entity, in this case God. In principle there is generally speaking more to be said for the conventional approach than for my approach, at least in relation to most matters. For instance it is very much easier for a person to set out to prove that elephants live wild in Africa (since one can go to likely places in Africa to observe elephants or at least evidence of elephants) than for a person to set out to disprove that elephants live wild in South America! (Elephants are a simple case compared to chimpanzees or even smaller animals.) However logical propositions are an exception to the generalisation that applies to empirical objects (i.e. that it is easier to demonstrate the existence than the non-existence of an entity). This is because something cannot exist if its very existence necessarily entails inconsistency and therefore logical self-contradiction. Therefore this opens the way to examining in a logical manner whether the concept of God entails logical inconsistency or logical self-contradiction in which case God does not exist. Of course if to disprove God's existence one had to show there is no empirical trace of God in the whole Universe, one might as well give up (or not start) on that since no human can empirically examine the whole Universe! However if one just has to look for logical inconsistency within the very concept of God to effect disproof, that effort is certainly worthwhile or at any rate reasonable. So my approach in looking for a logical disproof of God's existence is certainly unconventional and unorthodox – only very few people including perhaps ancient Sceptics and Charles Bradlaugh have ever tried it. However it does offer some prospect of being an appropriate approach to a logically based argument.

My third break with orthodox convention is to focus attention on ignorance rather than on knowledge. This approach would not occur to most people since people are generally brash and proud about their supposed knowledge and unwilling to admit to ignorance even where it exists. In a historical context arguments deriving from general ignorance are not unheard of. Gorgias of Leontini, the ancient Greek sophist (c485BC-c380BC) argued, 'Nothing can be known; even if anything can be known, nobody could know it; and even if anybody could know it, nobody could communicate it.' The ancient Sceptics were also quite fond of arguing that we are ignorant and so can be sure of little or nothing. However the subsequent increase in human knowledge has probably made people less willing to argue from ignorance. And intellectually Descartes (1596-1650) in his maxim 'cogito ergo sum' ('I think, therefore I exist') at last finally proved that contrary to Gorgias' maxim something can definitely be known. If only Gorgias had stated instead, 'There is no God; even if there was a God, it could not be known by anybody; and even if it could be known by anybody it could not be communicated with' – then Descartes could not have validly disproved his statement! Anyhow Gorgias had a good run of around two thousand years before his actual maxim was disproved but since the time of Descartes it has not been common to argue from the stance of ignorance. Furthermore the very concept of ignorance may seem especially inappropriate in relation to a potential God's alleged ignorance. But my insight is to actually question God's supposed omniscience and investigate in detail whether it can actually and logically ultimately be genuine. This is a strange thought and an unconventional thought and indeed an overlooked thought but I think ultimately a useful thought! Everything here hinges on the very nature of knowledge but I shall be bold and unlike other people not take for granted the notion of complete divine knowledge. Perhaps even to think of this shows insecurity and my unusual lack of the normal intellectual confidence but the result might also expose the concept of God's insecure position! Anyhow it is very unusual and unorthodox to argue about ignorance, especially in relation to God.

My fourth and final major piece of unorthodoxy is to deviate from the human point of view and look at things primarily from a potential God's point of view. It is admittedly reasonably common for thinkers to talk about things from God's point of view once they have supposedly established or at least assumed that God actually exists. Yet it is very uncommon, if not unheard of, for people to look at things from a potential God's point of view in arguments about the very existence of God. So I have innovated in a fundamental way because humans are finite and their knowledge of empirical matters is necessarily also finite which is very unlike a potential God who is supposedly infinite. Presumably a potential God is only constrained by the constraints of what it is possible, logically possible, to do. Therefore a potential God is only limited by logical possibility and not by merely mortal limitations, and it is such logical limitations that I will invite you to examine. In any event this approach of examining things from a potential God's rather than from a human point of view is unorthodox and rather innovative.

Of course the odd person has been unorthodox in one or more of these four respects but it is doubtful whether anybody has been unorthodox in all four of these respects.

How did I come to be so unorthodox? I don't really know. I suppose I don't think like most other people. Probably a dislike of the rituals and inconveniences of religion predisposed me to be an atheist, and then I looked for proof of it. Perhaps a scepticism over claims to knowledge made me willing to argue about ignorance. Yet looking at things from a possible God's point of view rather than from our own may have been sheer inspiration combined with some ability to see things in a detached manner.

Perhaps it is good fortune for such an unorthodox combination to succeed. But then again perhaps such a radically different approach opens up a whole new vista and therefore a whole new opportunity to take an entirely fresh look from a fresh approach to deal with an old problem. I myself think that this unusual approach, unusual in so many ways, to the problem of God's existence or non-existence has helped clear the way to solving the problem even if this combination of unorthodoxies may have been a lucky combination.

B. Summary Of The Argument

1. An uncertain God is a contradiction in terms.

2. Everything in the Universe must be fundamentally uncertain about its own relationship to the Universe as a whole because there is no way of attaining such certainty.

3. Therefore even an entity with all God's other qualities cannot have the final quality of certain knowledge concerning its own relationship to the Universe as a whole.

4. Therefore God cannot exist because even any potential God cannot know for sure that it is God.

Stated as a logical paradox in relation to a possible God this argument might be condensed into the statement, 'God cannot exist because God cannot know for sure that it is God.'

C. Explaining The Argument

Let us begin a search for an answer to the question whether God exists by examining the matter from our own human perspective.

The very first point I wish to make is that it is widely acknowledged that humans have been unable actually to prove the existence of any kind of monotheistic God. This is despite thousands of years of trying and despite countless professional apologists for many differing religions.

One may ask why is this? It could be because there is no God and therefore there cannot be any valid proof of God's existence. I believe this to be true. It could be that we humans are too stupid to find the proof, or even to recognise the proof that some people have found. However it could be that because of our human limitations, we humans who are necessarily finite cannot prove the existence of an infinite God, even if God actually exists. Let us examine this further.

For instance, suppose some entity happens to turn up and claims it is immortal. What does a mortal human or even a society of mortal humans do about it? Of course humans may question it a bit or a lot and that entity may or may not seem cooperative in response to that human questioning – that is its prerogative. In any case questioning is not likely to be logically conclusive about whether it is actually immortal or not. Certainly non-cooperation with humans or even lying to humans would be no proof of mortality or immortality! The next things humans might do assuming they are brutal enough and brave (given the entity's potential immortality and thus possible scope to harm us mortals) is that they might attempt to kill it and so show it is mortal. Assuming people can't kill it nor even harm it there is not much else mortal humans can do to test the claim of that entity to be immortal. I suppose people could wait for many years, even for many generations to see if that entity actually dies. But assuming it does not die, humanity could end up waiting until the last human has died and humanity is extinct without being able to know whether that entity which claims to be immortal is in fact literally immortal or not. I dare say in practice people, being opinionated though mortal, will eventually come to a belief over whether that entity is mortal or immortal. Yet that belief will tend to be based on its credibility and charisma in other matters, not upon its sheer prospects of mortality or immortality. However such a human view as to its mortality or immortality is a mere human opinion or conjecture, not in any way a proof nor even an indication of its actual mortality or immortality. Since human beings are not immortal, there is no possible way we humans can know that anything will not die, perhaps long after all human beings are dead! So there is no possible way that we humans can distinguish conclusively between what will just be extremely long lived and what is actually immortal. So there is no possible way that we humans can actually prove or even know for certain that any entity at all is immortal!

The same human limitation that prevents humans from identifying immortality also applies to humans identifying other qualities such as omniscience. If an entity chanced along and claimed to be omniscient there is no way humans could confirm that it is actually omniscient rather than just extremely knowledgeable. (Or perhaps if the entity is not cooperative – and there is no reason why a possibly omniscient entity has to be cooperative with the limited intellects of humans – we might not even be able to confirm that it is extremely knowledgeable). So (assuming it is at least credible and is not overcome by us) that entity might be omniscient or it might just be far more knowledgeable than us. Yet we humans being limited in our intellect have no way of distinguishing between these two possibilities! This argument so far is essentially the same as my previous Comprehension Gulf Argument but please be patient because I am soon going to take it further than I did in the Comprehension Gulf Argument and apply its logic even to a potential God.

So with humans being bound, inevitably bound to fail in matters of recognition, such as recognising the absolute quality of immortality, what if some entity came along and claimed to have all the qualities appropriate to God (immortality, omniscience, omnipotence and others)? Well, assuming that it was at any rate considerably more powerful than us humans, we would not be able to judge whether it was actually omnipotent, omniscient and eternal as well, let alone judge whether it was God. So as we could not determine whether this entity has absolute qualities, we humans could not physically distinguish between a real God and an impostor claiming to be God. Obviously if its ethical behaviour was atrocious or more than one entity claiming to have such qualities appeared, that might raise questions about any claimant's authenticity as God, irrespective of its sheer power. However assuming it was far more powerful than us a false God would not even need to be eternal but could make do with pretending to us humans that it is eternal. So we humans could not possibly in logical terms recognise God even if he appeared before us.

So just suppose that in the future – as we know this has not happened yet – some entity came and proclaimed to all mankind that it is God and it did expel belief in all rivals and all other religions from the Earth. Should humanity then believe that such an entity was God or even likely to be God? We should of course strictly speaking say that we as mere mortal humans are unable to truly know whether any entity that is far more powerful than us is indeed truly omnipotent, omniscient and eternal. However we could also point out that there can only ever be either one true monotheistic God or otherwise no true God but there might be thousands, millions or practically innumerable entities that are far more powerful than us – indeed so powerful that though they are merely powerful entities (or daemons) they are quite capable of acting as God to us. After all if they have significantly more power than us they can pretend to us (or even delude themselves into believing) that they are omnipotent, eternal, omniscient and indeed God. We humans being far less powerful than such daemons would probably have no way of knowing (other than by Logic) that they were not in fact God. Obviously if any such daemon was anything like the Scriptural Gods that insist upon being worshipped it might be as well for our own safety to acknowledge such an entity as God. But speaking truthfully there is no logical way for us finite humans to properly identify what exactly is an infinite God. We as humans being finite could not possibly distinguish between a much more powerful entity than us and God. However we might surmise there are likely to be many, perhaps millions, perhaps a countless number of entities throughout the length and breadth of the Universe fraudulently claiming to be God but either no or at most one actual God. So it is far more likely on any law of averages that any such entity one encounters is a fraud and not genuinely God. This is perhaps particularly relevant as in the past people have believed in many different Gods – so any genuine God can hardly be too concerned with banishing thoughts of rival pretender Gods away from minds, even human minds, everywhere in the Universe.

Indeed the thought might also cross one's mind that if one had sufficient power (but not omnipotence) it might be good entertainment or at least quite pleasing to parade oneself (albeit fraudulently) as God to lesser species. Many people would enjoy doing that if they could! Of course one might claim that uniting worlds in belief in one entity, even in oneself posing as God, is beneficial to the races that come to believe in oneself because it might bring them unity of purpose and make them behave better! Anyway, it is certainly possible to imagine millions of powerful daemons parading themselves as God to lesser entities in millions of different parts of the Universe. Even perhaps child daemons might entertain themselves with such a game of deceit just as we mere mortals might play Monopoly or Poker. They might feel secure in the knowledge that the lesser races such as humans are quite unable because of their limitations to distinguish their claims to be God from the actual God, if such exists. This could be all the more enjoyable given the possible propensity of lesser races (certainly if they are anything like humans) to neglect Logic and readily give unwarranted and certainly unprovable credence to their claims to be God. Indeed their amusement might be all the greater when one considers that they might not even need to parade themselves as God. They might merely parade some robot or even some image they had produced or had access to as God – then they might enjoy seeing some manufactured robot or image worshipped as the one almighty God among lesser races!

So it is absolutely impossible for even a genuine God to overcome human limitations so as to make finite humans logically certain of identifying a genuine God and distinguishing a genuine God from a fake version of God. Of course 'God' may affect our minds and cause us (albeit illogically) to believe in himself as God but then again a mere daemon (i.e. a very powerful entity) could also affect our minds and so cause us, albeit wrongly, to believe in it as God. What nothing is able to do is to provide logical proof to us finite humans that it is truly infinite, and also that it is truly God even if it were truly God – for that would be doing the logically impossible just like creating a square circle would be doing the logically impossible.

Having looked at things from the human point of view I now propose to look at things from the view of a potential God from where the view in many respects is very different, indeed often fundamentally different. So an effort of imagination will be required to see things from the point of view of a potential God. Some things, as I shall show, such as the possibility of sudden change do remain the same whether one be human or whether one be a potential God. However because of seemingly absolute power and seemingly absolute uniqueness etc some things can look very different if one is a potential God contrasted with what they look like when one is merely human. Nevertheless let us try to approach things from the point of view of a 'candidate' God, that is an entity that apparently seems to itself to have all the attributes of God but is not sure whether it is actually God (before it reviews its position!).

So let us first consider the nature and effects of the sheer uniqueness of a potential God and thereafter in various numbered sections other matters from the perspective of this notional 'candidate' God.

(i) The Unique Perspective Problem

God being monotheistic and omnipotent and indeed our ultimate creator must be unique if he is to be God. If there were more than one entity like him he would not be omnipotent (i.e. more powerful than everything else which must include anything even partially like him) and monotheistic (i.e. the only God). Nobody, or at least no monotheist would dispute that.

However uniqueness, especially this sort of uniqueness in one's fundamental characteristics does have its profound consequences. In particular we humans rely mainly on other humans to gather our knowledge: a potential God cannot rely on other Gods to gain its knowledge.

So far as uniqueness is concerned God would be in a worse position than a man stranded alone (like Robinson Crusoe) on a desert island. Not only would he not have other Gods there to speak with and to learn from but he would not even have the prospect of coming off his desert island and meeting others of his race again. Even worse, he would have no memory of life before being stranded alone nor of contact with others of his kind nor of anything beyond his desolation. In fact he would have no memory nor knowledge of the existence of anything of even vaguely his own kind. A 'candidate God' would necessarily have for ever to experience the ultimate in loneliness and isolation. Leaving aside any emotional difficulties this isolation might or might not cause even to a potential God, it necessarily causes considerable intellectual difficulties.

To help in understanding the intellectual difficulties caused by isolation let us contrast the intellectual experience of this 'candidate God' in his isolation with that of normal human beings. Human beings gain most of their knowledge (both practical and theoretical) not from within themselves nor from arriving at it unaided by themselves but from the instruction and observation of other human beings. People tend to use analogy from the situation and experience of similar entities, that is other human beings, and then apply it to the world in general and to themselves in particular. For example we know that breathing is essential to life primarily because other humans have discovered this and told us so. We know that we were born because we have the testimony of others that this was the case. We also know that we are going to die, not because we ourselves have died but because it has become recognised as a universal human experience – and each individual among us has become accustomed to recognising himself as one individual human being among a huge race of human beings.

Nobody is able to remember his own birth, let alone his development in the womb or early infancy. So because of the records of others, the memories of others and the analogy with other people, we accept that our own birth, development and infancy occurred. Otherwise we would be completely ignorant about our own genesis and early life. A potential God, by contrast being unique, cannot rely for this sort of knowledge upon the records and memories of other Gods or even any other entities. Indeed one can go further and say that our own human memory does not even function as far back as our birth or early life, let alone our conception and all that time so far as we are concerned is not even a blur but just a complete void. How therefore can even a potential God be sure that its memory is not also a complete void before a certain time and thus that it too did not at some time arise (like we humans do) in a way unknown to itself? I don't see how a potential God can conceivably have any means of being completely certain that this is not the case!

Indeed even in life we gain most of our knowledge from the information supplied to us by other people. For instance breathing is fundamental to life. Yet most of us only understand that we are breathing because other people endowed with medical and biological knowledge which we lack and probably would never have discovered for ourselves have told us that it is happening. It may seem obvious to us when we know it but we would probably never on an individual basis have discovered it on our own for ourselves. Another way in which we are assisted by the knowledge of others is in something so basic to our civilisation as the means of producing fire (from which heat and light naturally come). So by its very uniqueness a potential God loses the most essential element, that of building upon (and indeed even initially from infancy benefiting from) the discoveries and foundations of others, that has contributed to human knowledge! Just think how much we humans would need just to compensate for that loss even in our technological heritage – if it could ever be compensated for. Yet a potential God has somehow not merely to compensate for that loss but on its own has to have knowledge far more advanced than we shall ever have. Indeed with God because it necessarily eternally has been God it does not even have the opportunity for development (or childhood) which we have: it has supposedly been completely knowledgeable (i.e. omniscient) even from the very beginning. In terms of knowledge an awful lot, indeed an inconceivable lot, is being required of this isolated, unique entity, God!

Massive though the problems of birth and life would be for isolated humans, the problem of conceiving of, still more knowing about, death would surely be even greater, possibly insurmountable! Let us return to our man on a desert island, though this time imagine him isolated from all other humans throughout his life or at least throughout his living memory. He would not know nor even have good reason to believe that he is mortal and will die one day. He would have even less reason to think of death if there were no animals on his desert island, just plants from which he was feeding. So far as he was concerned his life which seems to have gone on for ever, and which he certainly cannot remember ever beginning would likewise continue on for ever into the future. We only think of death, or at the very least we only think that death is inevitable for all of us because we have heard from other people that everybody in recorded history has died in due course. Indeed many of our acquaintances, especially our older acquaintances, have actually died. But a potential God, at least a monotheistic God, is necessarily acquainted with no other Gods – so how can he possibly be certain or even confident from the experiences of others like him whether he will eventually die or not? Surely the truth of the matter must be that any entity in that isolated position (just like our isolated person on a desert island) cannot possibly be confident, let alone certain whether or not his existence will in due course come to an end. An isolated and so far as he knows unique entity whether it be a man on a desert island or whether it be a candidate God, can have no reliable evidence on which to base an assumption or even guess as to whether he is mortal or immortal. (Even change and decay which apparently God would not undergo is not very good evidence since change and decay could be cyclical and as we humans know very well some deaths such as those from heart attacks can be very sudden). So there is no way that an isolated and unique entity can actually be sure whether he is mortal or immortal. Indeed such evidence as there is, limited and possibly irrelevant though it may be since God would in some ways appear different to all other things, suggests that things tend to change and ultimately die and that all things are mortal. Anyhow, what I am saying is that from our human perspective we suppose we are mortal primarily because we are told and believe all other humans have historically been mortal. Yet a potential God from his perspective of being isolated and unique would not have the means of knowing as we humans do (i.e. by strong analogy) about whether he is mortal or immortal.

So being unique as God must be, means that in terms of knowledge in general and of self-knowledge in particular a potential God suffers from terrible disadvantages compared to us humans. His perspective is necessarily a lot more isolated and a lot more difficult than ours. Some communication with (and the experiences of) similar creatures is available to us but not available to a potential God. Obviously this means that though a candidate God being unique of his kind (so far as he knows!) is cut off from many routes to practical knowledge, he is of course not excluded from all means of gaining knowledge. For instance we humans do learn some things from our own experience and occasionally even from the experiences of other humans we observe. Of course if God is not only unique but omniscient and omniscient from the very beginning of time, there is no scope for his learning (i.e. adding to his already existent knowledge) from his own experience or from the experience of other lesser entities. But if one were to take a less rigorous, strict view of God's qualities, God might be able to learn something from his own and others' experiences over time. The Bible of course – as usual – has things both ways. In some parts God is omniscient, inscrutable and knows everything in advance. Yet in other parts of the Bible, generally the earlier parts where God is more anthropomorphic, God does indeed learn from his own experience and 'mistakes' such as when he destroyed mankind in Noah's time and started again so as to create things better the second time round. Be that as it may, scientific and technological discoveries are usually made through research and experiments and percolated (or distributed) through communication between us humans in society, rather than through merely examining the experiences of ourselves or even others.

Certainly we can gain some of our knowledge through our powers of reasoning and that naturally we might suppose would be God's strong suit. Obviously it can be argued by theists that God is the supreme master of reasoning and would know everything that can possibly be known by reasoning. How he might have acquired such powers of reasoning is of course a mystery. After all humans tend to be taught reasoning or at least develop their ability to reason with the help of experience. In practice reasoning does tend to be helped by and even develops to an extent from practical things such as pattern recognition – at least among humans. But God was somehow born with or rather always had reasoning powers! A computer which is made at a period in time and is taught or programmed by humans before springing into action may in some ways provide some comparison. However I doubt whether a potential God would care to think of itself as possibly being a fabricated and programmed device. Be that as it may, the knowledge that can be gained from reasoning is far from comprehensive and is severely limited. Reasoning cannot foresee either most irrational situations or scenarios where a choice may be exercised. So for instance if an uncertainty principle were to apply anywhere (such as Heisenberg's Uncertainty principle or indeed quantum mechanics) or perhaps even if an entity has some genuine freewill to choose then it is impossible to know everything by reason, or indeed I suspect by any other reliable means.

In conventional theory all knowledge arises either by a priori means based on reason or perhaps (arguably) reached by insight or more commonly by a posteriori means which is basically through the experience of either oneself or others. So a possible God being both unique and omniscient from the very beginning of time (or events) is effectively excluded from getting knowledge in the a posteriori way, which is in fact the main way in which knowledge is in practice gained by humans and other living creatures. So far as the other type of knowledge, a priori knowledge, is concerned God would admittedly be less handicapped by his unique position. This is because the handicap he suffers here, that of not having the time nor the help of teachers to develop an a priori reasoning ability, might be overcome by the overwhelming intelligence that God is necessarily assumed to have. However the problem with a priori knowledge that is inescapable is that it is limited to understanding the unavoidably rational and invariable elements of the Universe and thus has relatively little practical application or even use.

So the very uniqueness that is an essential element of a monotheistic God, although indispensable to omnipotence and consequently the aspect of God related to his absolute power, weakens our potential God in relation to his claim to omniscience. His uniqueness closes off the main channels through which knowledge is generally acquired by living entities in practice.

I will now proceed to examine some epistemological (or knowledge-related) problems that arise even when looked at from a potential God's point of view and which I suggest cannot be overcome even by a potential God. Failure to overcome such problems would mean that nothing, not even any potential God could be omniscient (and so he must suffer uncertainties, that is lack of omniscience) even though omniscience must be an essential characteristic of a monotheistic God.

(ii) The Eternity Problem

God by definition would have to be immortal or in other words eternal. But the problem is how can even a potential God absolutely know that he is eternal? There are considerable problems even with eternity into all the past but the problems of knowing one is eternal into the whole of the future are surely even theoretically insurmountable.

To consider the past first, the question is how can even a potential God be absolutely certain that he has existed throughout all previous time? How can it know for sure there was not a time before its earliest genuine memory when it did not exist? It is easy to imagine the simple claim a theist would probably make in answer to that question. He would probably say that it is easy for God to know that he has existed for all past time because he remembers or even knows it all. Just as humans know they lived in previous years because they remember it, God can know he existed through the whole of the past because he remembers it. Obvious really. As it's so simple people haven't really bothered to question it. But there are some possible problems as an analogy with anything, be it computers or humans would reveal.

First there is a possible problem with taking perception, memory or even knowledge as far back as the infinite past because with living things the further back one goes often the more things tend to blur, become faint even in memory and become inaccurate. Here in going back into the past we are not merely discussing going a long way back but going into an infinity. Isn't it possible that confronted with going back into an infinity, even a potential God might find its knowledge becoming faint, blurred and inaccurate? Can anything, even a potential God really cope with an infinity? It is hard to see how one, even a potential God can reasonably be absolutely confident about that.

The second problem is even worse. Memories, especially distant memories, even of a potential God might actually be illusory or false. For instance it may one day become possible for us to plant in animals or humans a false set of memories. Hypnosis on occasion already seems to do it. And there have apparently been cases of so called counsellors, certainly specialist paid 'professional' counsellors, managing to evoke false memories in adults of child abuse to themselves when they were children. In any event most people seem to subconsciously adjust their memories so as to believe what they want to believe or what it is convenient for them to believe. How then does even a potential God know for sure that his distant memories have not turned into illusion perhaps so as to believe in his own immortality which he so much wants to believe in? Or even more radically how can he be sure that at some point he has not been mentally tampered with and been the victim of false memories being implanted in him without his knowing it?

A third problem for a potential God is to be sure he is not something akin to a computer. Not being a computer expert, I am not entirely sure how computers work. However I suspect that though computers are more reliable than humans and their memory bank of events does not dim with distance in the same way that human memory does, they must hit some barrier or limit in what they can conceive of. They certainly do not remember back to the time when they were manufactured and assembled! In essence computers are only capable of certain types of memory. Efficient though computers may be, they are not competent nor even capable of dealing with certain topics of memory or time such as the distant past or how they themselves came into existence in the first place. Isn't it possible that even a potential God might be of that type and suffer the same kind of limitations? And anyhow how can a potential God actually be absolutely certain that this is not the case?

A fourth problem for a potential God is how can he be confident that he is not like animals or human beings and does not suffer a peri-natal memory void like we humans do? We humans are just incapable of remembering our own conception, our life in the womb, our birth or even our very early life. We just cannot remember it. Might not a potential God also suffer a memory void around such a time? And unlike us who are assured by other humans that such events which we cannot remember actually did occur, in his case there are no other Gods nor even entities to remember such events for him. Might not a potential God naturally in such circumstances therefore assume that any period covered by (and before) this possible memory void just never existed? How does a potential God know that even in his case his memory did not develop after he was born? This would mean that although his life did actually start at some point in the past, because of his memory void he just cannot remember back so far as his birth or even his early life. How can he actually know for certain that he is absolutely eternal rather than suffering from some memory void that blocks out the distant past before his birth as well as his birth and early life? I don't see how even a potential God can be absolutely sure of that!

So even in respect of the past I can see considerable problems that throw doubt on a potential God's claim to be eternal and immortal throughout the whole of the past – and I don't see any way in which a potential God could conceivably disprove or even dispel these doubts. However in relation to the future, a potential God cannot even rely on memory or knowledge of the past but has to substitute extrapolation into the future which is even worse. This presents a futurity problem that cannot be overcome.

The essence of the futurity problem is that the past cannot be relied upon to predict the future. There can be no certainty that things will not change either suddenly or even gradually in the near future, still less in the far distant future. So what seems immortal may not actually be immortal but may be subject to unforeseen change or even death in the future. Indeed the change may even be irrational rather than rational, uncaused rather than caused, but no less devastating for that. The point that the past cannot be relied upon to predict the future is not original. It has been made thousands of years ago by the Indian Carvaka school and also over two hundred years ago by David Hume. This point has often been ignored (after all it is human nature to suppose that what has happened regularly in the past will reliably continue to happen in the future) but it has never been successfully responded to. Indeed it is not merely not the past but actually nothing at all that can be relied upon to predict future events. Actually it is irregular events that are very often fundamental and decisive. For instance a man may not have a day's illness after childhood and yet after fifty years of good health suddenly suffer a heart attack and die both suddenly and unpredictably within a matter of minutes. To take another example nothing is supposedly more certain than that night follows day. Yet one day, albeit in perhaps five thousand million years, that won't happen because things will change and life on Earth – if it still exists then – may disappear forever. The regularity will be broken and the consequences may be cataclysmic. Even a potential God cannot be certain that the same sort of thing will not one day unpredictably happen to him. There is no way anyone or anything, even a potential God can be certain that a potential God's power or existence will not disappear at some time in the future. There is no conceivable technique of knowledge that could possibly provide absolute certainty of that. After all the future has not yet happened. Even if any supposedly reliable technique of knowing the future became available it could not be confirmed to be reliable for the whole future which of course has not yet been fully experienced and so has not been fully tested yet. Indeed nothing could ever be tested in relation to the whole future since the whole future will not have occurred at any time!

Perhaps I ought to mention that certain theists have suggested that eternity and immortality should be seen in a different way in relation to God than is normally the case. Their argument is perhaps ingenious but it is surely fallacious. Their fallacious suggestion is that God can and does exist outside time. It is now popular with modernist monotheists but the argument was actually put in ancient Roman times in the sixth century AD by Boethius (480-524AD). Anyhow the suggestion is that from a vantage point outside of time God eternally actually sees all time at the same moment as if everything really was happening at the same time. In this theory time is like a reel of cinema film and God like some projectionist merely has all the clips of film rolled out in front of him and timelessly sees the whole of it. No real evidence is ever put to substantiate this theory beyond it being a nice idea. The fallacies of this (Boethius') argument are first that it is wrong to see time primarily as other than a sequence of events (and the sequence in events cannot be abolished) and secondly it is fallacious to suppose that anything can exist outside time or outside the run or sequence of events. In any event just as the projectionist with his clips of film (who incidentally does live in his own time) is mortal, no entity can be sure of escaping mortality and eventual death. So even apart from the theory that anything including a potential God can be outside of time being unsubstantiated and fallacious, it would still not absolutely prove that whatever its relationship to time or other events may be any entity can be sure of continuing or existing forever. So even a potential God cannot in any way validly rebut an eternity problem, that is the possibility which it cannot logically discount that it may itself be merely mortal and cease to exist.

(iii) The Is There A World Beyond Me Problem?

In the fifteenth century European peoples learned about what must at the time have been something of a shock discovery, that there were extra undiscovered continents in the world beyond the seas which had seemingly previously marked the limits of the world. The conventional human knowledge of centuries, even millennia, was suddenly overturned by the discovery of some extra, hitherto unknown continents. The world suddenly seemed larger than people had previously imagined. In time the discovery of this larger area led to the discovery of novel things such as tobacco, novel animals and novel civilisations there. Yet great as the shock to the Europeans who discovered America was, I suppose the shock to the native Americans who lived there was even greater. From their point of view an unknown though more advanced civilisation with guns and better technology had landed in their midst from somewhere beyond the seas of their known world to rob them, kill them with previously unknown diseases and conquer the remnants of their societies through greater technological power.

Of course nowadays with ever advancing Astronomy and astronomical instruments it has become commonplace to discover ever more distant stars and galaxies. First, people started to discover extra further out planets in our solar system, Uranus in 1781, Neptune in 1846, Pluto in 1930 and even Charon as recently as 1978. Then ever more distant galaxies were discovered. Now previously undreamed of, yet radical features of the Universe such as Black Holes, dark matter and star nurseries are being speculated upon. Still there are continuing expectations in Astronomy that ever more and indeed more distant features remain yet to be discovered.

To return to our 'candidate God', how can he possibly be certain that there are not regions unknown to him beyond what he sees and understands yet to be discovered? How can he be absolutely sure that he will not eventually suffer the same fate as the pre-Columbian native Americans? Might he find that he is discovered, then taken over or destroyed by something coming from beyond the limits of the presently known Universe with a power and technology greater than that known to him? How can a potential God or any entity in his situation truthfully discount that possibility? After all we humans do not consider it absolutely impossible that we will be visited, overcome and taken over by a more advanced race from another area of Space. So how therefore could even a potential God be absolutely certain that he could never even in the distant future be 'visited', overcome and so displaced as God by an even greater power coming from a place which is beyond the known limits of the Universe and previously unknown even to him? Perhaps the Universe is in reality greater in extent than even our hypothetical God thinks it is! After all the prime method by which people or even a candidate God know the limits of the Universe tends to be their inability to see or perhaps even conceive beyond the presumed limits of the Universe which amounts to 'knowledge' through ignorance. That of course is not actually a good and reliable method for defining or determining the limits of the Universe! We could after all just live within one system (or cosmos) within a greater Universe that contains multiple systems, perhaps vastly separated from each other! How can we or even a potential God actually be certain that this is not the case? Inability to see or even recognise that other 'systems' exist is no proof that other 'systems' do not exist beyond ours! Perhaps a potential God is only supreme (perhaps only temporarily) in our 'system' but not in other systems beyond us which even he cannot see – in which case he might eventually be knocked off his 'God perch' by entities from other systems discovering and breaking into 'our system'. Obviously if he is only a supreme entity within one 'system' within the Universe instead of over all systems (the rest of which he is unable even to see) he cannot be God. Even if he cannot be absolutely sure whether other 'systems' exist beyond this system of which he is apparently master, he cannot be sure whether he is genuinely God or merely a local potentate! Indeed he surely can have no means of absolutely knowing whether there are indeed some worlds or some systems beyond the system which at the moment he seems to control as master.

Therefore the 'is there a world beyond me problem?' is yet another problem which undermines the status of any potential God and which there is no means of resolving logically. So in logical terms this is another problem which should cause even a potential God himself to have logical doubts about whether he is actually genuinely God.

(iv) The Limited Intelligence Possibility

The problem here is that nothing can be sure of not being limited in intelligence because limited intelligence might include even for a potential God the inability to see one's own limited intelligence. For instance if you are a person of limited intelligence it might be that precisely because you only have limited intelligence you cannot know that you are a person of limited intelligence – and more obviously it is quite likely that you would not understand how your intellect is limited. So it is perfectly possible for anything to be limited in its insight and because it is limited in its insight not have the least idea that it is limited in its insight. Let me illustrate this with a possible and picturesque example so as to elucidate the abstract reasoning here:

'Imagine a race somewhat more technologically advanced that mankind. They have already created 'test tube life'. Now they are determined to create a 'test tube mini-cosmos' – all in a milk bottle sized container. Of course the individual life forms and planets which come to exist within that container would have to be miniscule but that is no problem for their creators in the same way as scaling down photographic images is no problem for us. They do use a protective (perhaps illusion-making) device to ensure that their 'test tube' life forms do not know they exist within a test tube and of course cannot break out of it into the wider world.

Now in some test tubes this technologically superior race invent a 'god' to preside over the whole test tube and in its imagination and experience over the whole Universe while in other test tubes they do not do so. So surprise, surprise they have created 'gods' or rather test tube gods – creatures who seem to have all the attributes of God but imagine rather than know (for how could they possibly know?) that they are God over the whole Universe. Yet in fact they are limited to control over the internal machinations of a milk bottle sized test tube! But never mind, they can in turn create and even thereafter destroy their own test tube gods (test tubes within a test tube) in the size of what would pass to them (the intermediate life forms) as milk bottle size. And so on and so on.

So how can any candidate God conceivably know for certain that it is not a mere test tube god – incapable, though unwittingly so, of seeing beyond or even to the limits of its test tube? After all test tube gods are within their own domain indistinguishable from a real god. And there are likely to be millions upon millions of test tube gods but there cannot by definition be more than one real God. So even the otherwise real God – if there is such a thing – cannot conceivably know that it is the real God.'

So there is no way any entity can for instance know for certain that it is not living in a test tube, a test tube whose boundaries, or whose 'glass' it cannot detect. Such can be the case with men or 'apparent gods'. And even more important, nobody or no thing can know that it is not limited in its intellect! After all if it were limited, part of its limitation would <u>quite likely</u> be to fail to understand that it is limited. Therefore those than cannot 'see' limitations to themselves cannot know whether there are any limitations.

So looked at even from a potential God's point of view there is no possible escape from the problem that one can never know for certain that one is not limited in one's intellect because part of the limitations to one's intellect might be that one just cannot see any limitations to one's intellect! This is of course an even greater hazard for a potential God than for humans as other humans are often only too willing to point out one's limitations whereas a potential God being unique and solitary has no society of Gods to enlighten him about his limitations! Therefore even a potential God cannot be certain that it is not somehow limited in its intellect in some way it does not comprehend!

(v) The Nature Of Knowledge Problem

Knowledge is a rather strange phenomenon. It is highly valued among humans which is not surprising since it often yields great practical benefits when applied to practical problems. Knowledge has helped us to live in greater comfort; it has enabled us to light up the dark first with fire, then with electricity; and it has even greatly increased the average human lifespan. No wonder knowledge is so highly valued – we spend our whole lives, especially our childhood, trying to acquire knowledge. We deem knowledge to be the most important thing that each generation can pass on to future generations. And yet for all that when one examines it closely, knowledge is actually a very slippery, a strangely slippery thing. This is partly because knowledge is an abstraction although it can often be used to deliver practical concrete results. It is also partly because knowledge may seem somewhat fickle in nature for the most part, at least over time and none can be entirely sure of grasping it fully. And however powerful or knowledgeable one may become knowledge as such apparently does not change its essential abstract nature to be more concrete or more easily held or less seemingly whimsically changeable – and those problems concerning the nature of knowledge may apply even to a potential God.

Having described the broad picture of knowledge, I would like to go into slightly more exact detail. In essence knowledge is always an abstraction, albeit an abstraction that can sometimes be adapted for practical use. However there are two fundamentally different types of knowledge, a small unchanging element of knowledge and a massive ultimately variable element of knowledge comprising the rest. To draw an analogy, the Universe is something like a kaleidoscope wherein the structure (or in a computer parallel the hardware) remains constant and unchanging but the pattern which can be seen (or in a computer parallel the software) is forever changing. This is just a useful analogy to illustrate the situation but it should not be pushed too far beyond illustrating that like a kaleidoscope the Universe has both an unchanging element and a changing element. In terms of the Universe some types of knowledge like pure mathematics and sheer logic (such as Descartes' maxim – 'cogito ergo sum' – 'I think therefore I exist') are surely always applicable and unchangeable. Unfortunately such knowledge has the limitations of being very limited and of being theoretical rather than essentially practical. The other type of knowledge which encompasses practical knowledge is changeable or at least potentially changeable. For instance even continents and stars change position over time: in fact in the end stars ultimately cease to exist as stars. Even viruses may in time evolve to become resistant to medicines such as penicillin. Indeed even the world which is seemingly predominantly rationally ordered or rationally arranged may at some time become predominantly irrational. We live in a world, indeed in a Universe, prone to change, albeit sometimes to change after a very long time and therefore all the happenings (or the patterns) within the world are merely provisional. In practice knowledge, even Science, tends to arise from the recognition and prediction of patterns in the Universe. And human nature being what it is, people tend to see a long repeated pattern as an invariable pattern which may even be developed into some scientific law. Yet when looked at from a long term point of view any such knowledge is only provisional knowledge. Such 'knowledge' lasts only until it is superseded either by some even better (or more popular) theoretical understanding of the Universe (or that part of the Universe) or by a change in the behavioural patterns within that section of the Universe itself. To bring it down to examples, Newtonian physics became accepted knowledge and survived as accepted knowledge until it was in part superseded by Einstein's theories which are themselves being refined and superseded – all this without the physical world changing. It is in this instance merely our knowledge of the Universe that is developing. However on occasion it is the world itself that does change and which acts as the cause of the change or variation in our knowledge. For instance the coastline of Britain (or indeed other countries) is in fact gradually changing and that is causing a change in our geographical knowledge, as conveyed through maps. So all this sort of knowledge as well as being abstract is indeed provisional upon either our understanding of the perceived phenomena or else upon the perceived phenomena themselves not changing. True, it may seem from the perspective of a potential God that his own interpretations are already perfect and will not change. However nothing, not even a potential God can guarantee that the perceived phenomena (including itself in the case of a potential God) will not themselves change at some time in the future, perhaps in a sudden, even irrational and completely unpredictable way, thus destroying the validity of that aspect of knowledge. From a potential God's point of view the world is under control, his control, but he has no possible means of knowing that the world will not somehow and irrationally at some point in the future go completely out of control, out of his control. This is because knowledge is an abstract concept which is usually only very tentatively and provisionally held on to by the 'knowers', be they human or potentially divine. Present knowledge, especially any practically useful knowledge, in no way guarantees the future pattern of the Universe. To know something, except where that knowledge is wholly logical and in general therefore of only theoretical use, is to have a present grasp of the present pattern and behaviour of that thing. To know something is emphatically not to have any guarantee of the future (especially the distant future) of that thing.

Knowledge therefore is generally provisional and even a potential God with logically maximal knowledge cannot overcome the essentially provisional nature of most knowledge. In particular nothing can have anything by way of guarantee through knowledge that existing patterns will not change and that he himself as a phenomenon will not in future die or even lose power as part of that changing pattern of things. Knowledge cannot guarantee one's continuing status within the Universe – it may often be a help but it is not a guarantee. So the very nature of knowledge as an abstract and mainly provisional phenomenon must apply to a potential God just as much as to us or to anything else. Even a potential God cannot guarantee his own future nor his present status as the genuine monotheistic God even through the application of all his knowledge. Knowledge itself is too limited, too weak, indeed too provisional, too illusory (and too slippery) a phenomenon to permit that. So a potential God cannot properly be said to 'know' that he is actually God. This is not merely because of possible deficiencies in God himself but also because the deficiencies inherent in the very concept of 'know' will not allow the concept of 'knowledge' to stretch into a guarantee of one's future status within the Universe – for that is beyond the very scope of 'knowing' or 'knowledge'.

(vi) The Uncertainty Problem

In essence what I am arguing is that every entity, be it a human being, be it a potential God is if it thinks seriously about it necessarily fundamentally uncertain about its own relationship to its environment. Such fundamental uncertainty must necessarily be universal. It must therefore be particularly acute for a potential God since its very status as a possible God is therefore in doubt. It is of course different in degree for us humans because we know that we are nothing much, each one of us being merely one fallible human among many humans that was born, lives and is destined to die. So questions of a cosmological or fundamental nature are really too long term and too remote to have a real impact upon our human lives in practice since the next payment of money to keep us happy for the next period of time tends to be more important to us. However when looked at from the perspective of a potential God these questions are far more significant since they affect whether it is really possible that he can actually be God or not! For instance we know – or strongly believe – we are not immortal but the question of whether he is mortal or not is fundamental not only to a potential God's prospects of eternal life but also to the question of whether he might actually be God or not because one cannot have a mortal God that will eventually die!

So let us look more closely at this uncertainty problem which we have already touched upon as being the situation in respect of a potential God's immortality, geography, intelligence and knowledge. In particular let us examine whether there is any conceivable way in which this problem which is proving such an obstacle to a potential God might genuinely be overcome. Obviously when looked at from a human perspective there can indeed be no means known or even knowable to mankind of proving anything is immortal or that there is no world beyond the limits of what one understands or that anything is not limited in its intelligence – but surely might not things be different in a way unknown to mankind from a divine perspective? Isn't it at least possible that all human uncertainties might be soluble and resolved by a divine entity? Of course it has to be readily admitted that neither myself nor other humans have reached the limit of practical wisdom nor even possibly of theoretical wisdom on this matter – but how can any entity conceivably know for certain that it has actually reached the limit of wisdom even if it thinks it has done so and even if it has advanced far further than us? We come down to the problem mentioned earlier to which I think there can never be any positive resolution. That problem is how can any entity, however advanced it may be, actually know for certain that it is not limited in its intellect or scope because part of its limitations could well be that it just cannot see any limitations to its intellect or scope? I think this point is in the end decisive. It means that one can never be sure that any solution (however neat any solution may seem) to problems (other than purely logical problems) that one has devised (especially in respect of one's own relationship to one's environment) is necessarily a final solution to the problems. Therefore in the end some element of uncertainty must necessarily remain. Therefore uncertainty triumphs here. Therefore all things, including potential Gods must necessarily exist in a Universe where the ultimate prospect must necessarily be uncertainty about the real nature of things now and even more so for the future!

(vii) The Logic Of Why Even A Potential God Would Have To Be An Agnostic

Before summarising the situation from a potential God's point of view I ought to state that in hypothesising a potential God, a seemingly eternal, omnipotent, omniscient, supremely good and controlling entity, I do not wish to imply that such an entity, a potential God that created and controls our world, actually exists. I do not myself think such an entity exists or is in fact anything more than a remote possibility (and there are grounds for saying such an entity even if it did otherwise exist could not be supremely good anyhow!). However I am here concerned to prove that even if such a potential God entity did exist at the very pinnacle of power and existence, indeed even if the greatest conceivable entity did now exist, it could not possibly actually be God! The argument I am putting here is that even the greatest conceivable entity in the Universe (let alone the greatest entity that actually does exist in the Universe!) must necessarily fall short of being God. This is because even it could not be sure of having or retaining for ever supreme power and intelligence over the whole Universe! That said, let us return to considering the position of this hypothetical candidate God who seems to have the attributes of God but is considering whether it can genuinely be God.

This potential God thinks it has lived for ever in the past but has no way in which it can be certain that it will live for ever in the future or know whether it might die (from the daemonic equivalent of a human heart attack or of a stellar explosion or whatever) at some time in the future. It must in logic therefore be agnostic on the question whether it is truly immortal. In fact it cannot even be absolutely certain that it has actually lived through all past time. Maybe it can only genuinely remember back to a certain point in time beyond which it may have either illusory memories or a peri-natal memory void (like us humans)! So a potential God's agnosticism about his possible immortality is further reinforced.

This potential God would also appear to hold his domain over the full extent of Space, that is the whole Universe and would seem to be omnipresent. But can he be sure that he is genuinely omnipresent?

Well, no. He does not know for sure that there is not some boundary (like the sea for earlier peoples) that he cannot cross or indeed that he cannot even see (like the alleged 'glass ceiling' on promotion for women). There may indeed be cosmological systems well beyond him that he is incapable of reaching – and since that is a possibility he cannot logically entirely discount he is forced to be agnostic on this point also.

Even in respect of whether he controls everything as he seems to, he is driven to agnosticism on this point too. This candidate God may think he does everything out of his own choice, but how can he be absolutely sure that he is not somehow restricted in his wishes to doing only those limited things he can manage to do? Or even worse how can even a candidate God be absolutely sure that all his actions which he thinks he does voluntarily arising from his own wishes are not in fact the result of being 'programmed' like some computer by something else and are only disguised to seem like his wishes? When confronted with this possibility, even a candidate God has no way of being absolutely sure that this is not so and that in fact he is ultimately 'controlling' not only the Universe but even his own actions. So our beleaguered candidate God must actually be agnostic even about this point too.

Of course our candidate God may think he is unlimited in his knowledge and on the face of it he is. He sees no rivals in knowledge to himself and he sees no limits to his own knowledge. But how can he in fact be certain that his knowledge is truly unlimited especially as one of the limitations to his knowledge might be an inability to see limits to his knowledge? There is no way even a potential candidate God can be absolutely certain of this. This knowledge problem (of not knowing one is not limited in intellect with inability to see one's limitations being one of the limitations) is logically just insoluble. So even a potential God cannot solve it and therefore must be agnostic over whether his knowledge is limited.

Therefore this potential God must necessarily be genuinely agnostic about quite a lot. In fact he must be agnostic about whether he possesses or even can possess many of a real monotheistic God's essential characteristics – immortality, omnipotence, conscious control, unlimited knowledge, unlimited intelligence and unlimited scope. All this is demolishing his supposed 'omniscience'.

So I have established here that any potential God must at best be an agnostic over whether he is actually God. Even from his own seemingly unique perspective of apparently unlimited existence, scope and power, a potential God, any potential God would (like human beings) have to ultimately be agnostic about whether his powers were real or artificial, permanent or temporary, unlimited or limited and so whether he was genuinely God or merely a very powerful daemon. So anything in this position, including an entity who actually was immortal, consciously controlling, limitless and supremely powerful, could not be entirely sure that he was in fact genuinely eternal, consciously controlling, limitless and supremely powerful. So even an entity whom we would otherwise be entitled to call God would have to be an agnostic!

The next and final part of the argument in developing this disproof of the existence of God through The God Paradox is in getting from the position that even a potential God would have to be agnostic about whether he is actually God to a proof that God cannot actually exist at all.

Obviously while it is reasonable for humans to be agnostic, it is on the face of it plainly absurd if even a potential God has necessarily to be an agnostic. If a candidate God cannot rationally believe in God, then surely nothing can rationally believe in God.

A consequence of any entity, even an apparently eternal, omnipotent, controlling and unlimited entity not being certain that it will exist for ever or indeed not knowing with certainty the full extent of the Universe is that even though it is itself a candidate to be God it simply cannot identify God. In effect it is suffering an identification problem with God similar to the identification problem with God that we humans suffer. Because there is no way that it can distinguish for certain even in respect of itself between what is mortal and what is immortal (even if it is going to live for ever, it hasn't yet lived for ever and so cannot be certain that it will live for ever), it too cannot definitively identify God. Because there is no way that even it can distinguish for certain between great scope and unlimited scope, it too cannot definitively identify God. Because there is no way that even it can distinguish for certain even in respect of itself between what is extremely powerful and what is actually omnipotent, it too cannot definitively identify God. So even if this entity actually were God in respect of its immortality, power, supreme goodness and other qualities it would still have an identification problem. It would still not be able to be certain in identifying itself as God because so far as it was concerned there would still be at least the hypothetical possibilities that it would in time die or be overpowered by some force beyond its control and so in the end turn out not genuinely to be God after all. It is bad enough if humans need to have 'faith' to believe in a God, but haven't we reached total absurdity if even God needs to have 'faith' to believe in God? Fortunately this conundrum can be resolved because I am now in a position to show that nobody need have faith in the existence of God because God is a logical impossibility and just cannot exist.

You may recall that one of a genuine God's essential qualities is 'omniscience'. This must be so. I asked earlier how can an entity be God if it is not omniscient and so is not fully aware of what is going on in the Universe, and so might for instance be unaware of whether there is some greater entity lurking somewhere unbeknown to it in the Universe? This point is irrefutable. Not being omniscient would be like trying to complete a jigsaw with some of the pieces missing – indeed in the absence of omniscience not even knowing the full size of the jigsaw. It could be a hopeless task especially if some of the missing pieces are so important that they transform the whole significance and interpretation of the jigsaw. Perhaps more pertinently God not being omniscient could be like claiming to govern a whole country when one's actual knowledge and control extended to only one county. To say the least that would make one very vulnerable to being attacked and overpowered from outside one's county. So there can be no real question that God (if God exists) absolutely must know everything that is going on everywhere and so be omniscient in order to be God – otherwise he effectively is not God.

But it is impossible, absolutely impossible for any potential God to be omniscient if he ultimately and fundamentally cannot know for certain that he is genuinely immortal, omnipresent, unlimited, omnipotent and consciously controlling. Yet I have already shown that no entity, not even any potential God can within the parameters of Logic possibly know for certain that he is genuinely immortal, omnipresent, unlimited, omnipotent and consciously controlling even if he may seem to himself and others to be all those things. Therefore I have shown that nothing, not even any potential God can possibly know everything and so be omniscient. So in the absence (which I have proved) of the quality of omniscience which is essential to a monotheistic God there can be no monotheistic God. So it is proved that the conventional God of monotheism cannot exist. It is logically and definitively proved that God does not exist (since if God cannot exist, God of course does not exist).

So this God Paradox (i.e. 'God cannot know for sure that it is God') shows that God cannot exist. In essence the argument has been to show with inexorable logic that nothing, not even a potential God can even know (let alone identify and attribute to any entity) whether some of the essential defining qualities of God such as immortality and omnipotence actually exist in respect of any entity. Therefore in the absence of such knowledge omniscience (which is necessarily an essential defining quality of a monotheistic God) cannot exist. Furthermore in the absence of any entity being able to be omniscient, no entity can have at least that one of the essential defining qualities of God and so no entity can be God and so God cannot exist.

What I am proclaiming is that unavoidable universal agnosticism is in fact an equivalent of atheism. This equation, the equation of universal agnosticism (which I have already proved) with atheism is the final piece in the jigsaw in disproving the existence of God through this argument.

If humans are agnostic, even necessarily agnostic because of their limitations as humans that does not in itself serve as an absolute disproof of God's existence (although it is a good reason for people not actually to believe in God), nor does it have any implications that spread wider than humanity. But if every entity including even any entity who would otherwise qualify as a candidate for being God (because of his seemingly unique and apparently supreme position within the known Universe) must also necessarily be agnostic as to whether any entity (including possibly himself) can be God, then that is equivalent to showing there can be no God at all. If no entity, not even any otherwise likely candidate to be God, could ever possibly have the definite knowledge of his own omnipotence and his own immortality that are essential to God, then indeed no entity can be God and God cannot exist. Human ignorance is one thing but universal ignorance is indeed another thing. Human ignorance is agnosticism but universal ignorance is atheism.

So with the revelation that inescapable universal ignorance of whether some of God's essential qualities can exist anywhere (and so whether anything can be God), is atheism, I have the final piece in this proof. I have now finally and irrefutably proved the non-existence of God.

D. Possible Objections To The Argument

So I have put and developed the argument that the thesis that God exists necessarily entails a paradox, the God paradox (i.e. that God would have to be omniscient and yet any potential God could not have any possible means of being sure that it is God). I claim this paradox can only be avoided by the thesis that nothing can be omniscient, therefore nothing can be God and therefore God does not exist. In short this argument is an absolute disproof of the existence of God.

However one can understand that many people, including of course priests and theologians whose livelihoods depend upon the alleged existence of God or at least upon the possibility of the existence of God, will wish to examine possible ways in which my argument might be invalid or at least open to doubt. Obviously I cannot even before this particular argument has been publicly debated guarantee to consider in advance every possible line of objection that might be raised against my argument. However I can and will examine some of the most likely objections that might be raised against my argument of Universal Uncertainty and The God Paradox. Some of the possible objections (such as ii and iv) are suggested by the critical points inherent in the argument itself. Some possible objections (such as i and vi) are indicated by the lines of argument monotheists themselves have used in relation to other arguments concerning possible weaknesses in the monotheistic case.

I shall proceed to consider six possible objections to my argument under a numbering system of (i) to (vi). Certainly these seem to be the most obvious points one can make in relation to my argument. I hope to show by demonstrating that none of these points is capable of undermining or even weakening my argument just how strong and well founded the argument I have developed for disproving the existence of God really is.

So without further ado, let us look at the possible objections.

(i) Scepticism Is Self Defeating

It has been argued by some religious apologists in relation to other generally sceptical arguments concerning the existence of God that sceptical arguments fail because to be consistent there must be scepticism about all things and scepticism about scepticism itself. For instance McDowell & Stewart wrote in their book Understanding Secular Religions (Page 30 – Refutation of Scepticism) as follows – 'Scepticism is ultimately meaningless. It refutes itself. If one declares "You can never be sure about anything" he is catching himself in his own trap. If we can be sure of nothing, then we cannot be sure of the statement "nothing is certain". But, if that statement is objectively true, then we can be sure about one thing, the statement. But if we can be sure about the statement, then the statement is false. If the statement is false, then we can be sure. The inexorable fate of the sceptic is to be condemned by his own sentence.'

Well, I suppose the main thing that piece of reasoning demonstrates is that the thoroughly sceptical position is better expressed as 'the only thing you can be sure about is that you can never be sure of anything else' rather than by the statement 'you can never be sure about anything' which I think may entail that self-contradiction. However my argument does not entail comprehensive scepticism about everything, which at least since the time of Descartes' examination of comprehensive doubt seems to be an untenable position anyhow. I do not dispute I can know, as Réne Descartes (1596-1650) knew, with certainty that I exist ('cogito ergo sum' – I think, therefore I exist) but what we cannot know is our place in the context of the Universe as a whole. I am arguing for a particular yet universally applicable uncertainty concerning any entity's relationship to the Universe as a whole so far as the entity itself is concerned. No entity can be absolutely certain how extensive the Universe (the totality of existence) is in Space or how long things will continue in their present mode. So my argument is not based fundamentally upon an axiomatic principle of comprehensive uncertainty nor even upon scepticism but upon Logic. It is the logic that is the primary principle that leads necessarily to a certain amount of unavoidable uncertainty. So uncertainty concerning one's relationship to the Universe as a whole is merely derivative from inexorable logic. Sheer logic is not in principle uncertain. Only that which is liable to change or potentially liable to change or susceptible to different possible explanations is uncertain. Therefore it is ineffective and incorrect to attack my argument as if it were an argument of total scepticism. It is not. It is also wrong to attack my argument as if it were an argument in which Scepticism is axiomatic. It is not – the scepticism is merely derivative of Logic, Logic which is axiomatic to the argument. So if my argument is to be confronted in an intellectual or sensible manner, either the validity of Logic as an axiomatic basis for argumentation, or my application of Logic would have to be questioned and found deficient. Scepticism may indeed if it is absolutely comprehensive or axiomatic be logically self defeating or unsustainable. However Scepticism enters into my argument neither as a comprehensive notion nor as an axiomatic principle but merely insofar as it is a consequence of Logic (which can prove that nothing can be absolutely certain of its ultimate place in or relationship to the Universe as a whole). Therefore my argument is not affected by the logical shortcomings of comprehensive or axiomatic scepticism (which in any event occur when comprehensive Scepticism is adopted prior to Logic rather than as in my argument when some Scepticism is found to be the result of the application of Logic).

(ii) There Might Be A Route To Certainty (Unknown To Us)

The possible objection here is that it may be arrogant to assume that just because we humans do not know any way of attaining certainty in such matters as the possible existence and identification of God, that necessarily means there is no way of attaining such certainty. It could perhaps be argued a more advanced entity, or indeed God himself could certainly recognise God.

Obviously I would not wish to claim that we humans are in possession of every means of attaining every sort of knowledge. But then neither can it rightly be conceded that any entity however powerful or knowledgeable it is, including a potential God, can properly possibly be absolutely certain that it itself is in possession of all knowledge both now and in the future and in every part of the Universe. So therefore the uncertainty of the position of any entity in relation to the Universe as a whole must remain. There is no way of cognising certainty. Put another way, there is no way for any entity to be absolutely certain that it has grasped the full situation properly and that it has not been let down because of its possible limitations that are unknown even to itself. I would even suppose that unless a scenario (such as my thinking and yet not existing) is genuinely logically self-contradictory, there can be no absolute certainty as to what is in fact ultimately the case. Furthermore no entity can be absolutely certain that it itself has achieved full and correct knowledge and is itself not somehow limited in its intellect and power.

So I admit we humans cannot be sure that techniques for attaining knowledge that are beyond our own knowledge or even comprehension do not exist. However this is not a valid objection to my argument against the existence of God because no entity, however advanced that entity may be, can be absolutely certain that yet further techniques for attaining or indeed undermining knowledge that lie beyond even its comprehension do not exist. So therefore universal uncertainty in respect of any entity's relationship to the Universe as a whole must remain. Therefore this particular objection cannot make any impact against my disproof of the existence of God.

(iii) Logic Has Limited Validity And Should Not Be Taken As Axiomatic

The possible objection here is whether Logic is really so universally reliable and applicable that it can properly be used in an axiomatic way in an argument of such universal and practically boundless scope as an argument concerning the possible existence or non-existence of God is likely to be. The monotheist might reasonably inquire whether my argument is indeed vulnerable at its logical core.

In response to that point my clear view is that Logic is universally valid and is valid however capricious or even irrational the world as a whole may seem or become. Frankly, it is inconceivable to me that it could be otherwise. For instance it is inconceivable to me that there is any type of world or part of the Universe where one could possibly think without existing in some form and therefore Descartes' logical maxim ('cogito ergo sum' – 'I think, therefore I exist') did not apply. For me it is even inconceivable that anywhere one may go, a straight line is at least theoretically anything other than the shortest distance between two points in space. I believe there may well be places and times in the Universe where our present physical 'laws' break down and disappear. There are pretty certainly instances where the nexus of causality (e.g. that somebody puts on a bandage because he was hit by a stone which occurred because another person threw that stone which itself occurred for some reason etc, etc) breaks down into sheer irrationality. Yet I still believe that Logic must be applicable even if causality within the events of the Universe breaks down and even if the present physical laws of the Universe either change or disintegrate altogether. I can well see that events within the Universe or at least large parts of the Universe might become irrational and unpredictable. (This would make it very difficult for life forms to live and exist at all since living things tend to rely on adapting to a situation that is predominantly repetitive, routine and therefore predictable.) But I cannot see even in those circumstances of unpredictability and irrationality how at least elementary Logic can cease to apply (at least theoretically). I cannot see how even conceivably propositions that are inherently mutually contradictory or self-contradictory or logically contradictory (such as being able to think without actually existing for instance, or to cite another instance being genuinely square and being genuinely circular at the same time) can possibly be valid or could possibly apply, however irrational the pattern of the Universe may be or may become. I therefore strongly believe that Logic is and must be universally applicable in all circumstances, whatever the real state of the Universe or part of the Universe may be at any given time. It would therefore follow that my argument is in no way defective nor at fault in taking Logic as axiomatic in the Universe and in arguing according to the precepts of Logic.

However, even if I am wrong about the efficacy of Logic throughout the Universe, the monotheist would in the end be in no better a position and a monotheistic God still could not exist. Let us try to think the unthinkable for a few moments and try to conceive the inconceivable, that is a scenario in which Logic is not necessarily applicable for all time throughout the whole Universe. I would find it hard to envisage a Universe (or a part of the Universe) where Logic was inapplicable but I can describe the resultant effect readily enough. It would be that we were deprived of our most reliable means of knowledge, and our only means of achieving a priori knowledge. So if Logic were eliminated (whether it be by our voluntary supposition or by force of circumstances or even argument), so too would be eliminated our chances of saying anything absolute, indeed anything more than what is very provisional about the ultimate nature of the Universe or the ultimate reality in which we live. We could then go back well over two thousand years for our philosophy and have to agree with Gorgias of Leontini (c485BC-c380BC) who claimed that nothing can be known and anyhow we have no way of knowing anything. In such circumstances we humans would in the first instance be agnostics about the possible existence of God, being even more unable than at present (when we may be assisted by Logic) to know whether God exists or not. But then even a potential God in the absence of a reliable Logic would seem to have even less prospect (if it is possible to have less than a zero prospect which is why I used the word 'seem'!) of knowing in the first place whether any God actually exists and in the second place whether he is actually God! Indeed if Logic were invalid or unreliable even a potential God would have even less grounds that he would in a logical Universe for being confident of his real extent or his future power! So in an ultimately illogical system or Universe, not only would we humans be in a worse position that we are in already but so too a potential God would also be in an even worse intellectual position (not to mention a physically even more vulnerable position!) than he is in already! I have already shown that it is not possible for any entity to be justifiably confident of his own relationship to the Universe as a whole if the Universe accords with logical canons. Yet it is even less possible (if that is feasible!) for any entity to be justifiably confident of his own relationship to the Universe as a whole if the Universe is not even necessarily subject to any logical constraints! In the circumstances of the Universe existing beyond the bounds of Logic, any knowledge, particularly any absolute knowledge, is even less possible for any entity that it is now in at least a logically constrained Universe. So it is quite impossible in an illogical Universe for anything to know that he has the qualities, most particularly omniscience, required of a monotheistic God and so it is quite impossible for any entity to know that it is God. So even in an illogical, irrational system or Universe, no entity would be able to genuinely know with certainty that it is God and self evidently therefore a monotheistic God could not exist. After all if one were to abandon the requirements for omniscience and knowing that one is the sole God even in an illogical Universe, one would also have to abandon the requirement for monotheism – since without absolute and reliable knowledge of there being no other God perhaps any one of a possibly huge number of powerful daemons could reasonably claim to be God. But of course the requirement of exclusivity as God or monotheism cannot be abandoned by monotheists even in an irrational Universe because monotheism is the main point of their religion and their belief!

So even if Logic was hypothetically found to be inapplicable to the whole Universe, a monotheistic God still could not exist (since no entity could even then have God's essential quality of omniscience)! So although Logic is indeed used as the basis and method of my argument, the only alternative which is an abandonment of Logic would also unavoidably lead to an atheistic conclusion. Therefore this objection to my argument, founded upon challenging its basis of Logic, is both hard to conceive of as being valid and also even if it were perversely actually to be valid it would not affect the end result which is inexorably atheism. Atheism is the only sustainable view both if the Universe is always amenable to Logic and also if the Universe is not always amenable to Logic!

(iv) Might The Way Logic Is Used In This Argument Be Incorrect?

The question to be examined here is whether, granted that Logic is an appropriate device, I have actually argued my case for the disproof of God's existence in a logically impeccable way. Obviously not only has the concept of Logic got to be appropriate but also the use of Logic has to be correct if my argument is to be valid. The question one may ask by way of objection here is whether Logic has been correctly applied in all the stages of this argument.

My submission is that Logic has been correctly used in all the stages of this argument. Obviously the simpler the argument is, and the fewer logical stages there are, the less scope there is for logical mistakes. So therefore it is sensible in logical terms to reduce the argument to its simplest valid form and its fewest logical stages. So reduced, my argument for the non-existence of God amounts to this:

1st Premise: If (a monotheistic) God were to exist, God would have to be omniscient.

2nd Premise: Nothing can be omniscient.

Conclusion: Therefore (a monotheistic) God cannot exist.

Clearly the logic by which the conclusion here follows necessarily from the two premises (if those premises are correct) is logically indisputable, so indisputable that it cannot be otherwise. If nothing can be omniscient and a potential God would have to be omniscient, nothing could be God and so God cannot exist. That logic cannot be faulted.

All that logically remains having shown that the conclusion follows logically and inexorably from the two premises is to demonstrate logically that each of the two premises is correct.

The first premise, that if a monotheistic God existed it would have to be omniscient, is relatively simple to show. Of course the great philosophers such as Descartes and Locke (and even Maimonides via the negative way) who have listed God's necessary qualities have all stated that one of a monotheistic God's essential defining qualities is his omniscience. Yet that is incidental since one cannot validly argue by agreement even with eminent authorities – one has to establish the point for oneself. However the basic point is not merely that a God limited in its knowledge would seem absurd. Yet more to the point a God that was not omniscient would not know for certain that it was eternal even if it was eternal, that it was the real controller over the whole Universe even if its control extended to the whole Universe and perhaps most to the point that it was unrivalled in power (i.e. monotheistic) even if it was unrivalled in power. In the absence of omniscience a potential God would have no way of knowing for sure that another God (or potential God) was not lurking somewhere unbeknown to it, able and perhaps ready to supersede its power. Therefore a monotheistic God would have to know the whole extent of the Universe (i.e. the totality of things) in both Space and Time to be entirely sure that it was genuinely God – without that certainty no entity could be God. So I submit that it is logically established beyond any doubt that the first premise (i.e. 'if a monotheistic God were to exist it would have to be omniscient') is correct and entirely valid.

The second premise, that nothing can be omniscient, is rather more general and sweeping and is at first glance less easy to establish. Obviously if a statement such as 'nothing can be certain that it is immortal because nothing can be certain of knowing the future' is correct, then this second premise would indeed be correct. However universal uncertainty about the future though on the face of it a reasonable and indeed correct enough principle is quite difficult to establish and prove in a logical form. Perhaps a sensible method of achieving such a proof is by translating it into a negative version of the point thus – 'There is no proven technique of knowing all the future, especially as any such potential technique cannot be fully tested nor known to be fully reliable until the entire future has actually occurred. Furthermore there never will be a time when all the future has occurred and therefore when any technique has been fully tested. Therefore no entity can be certain of knowing all the future. Therefore no entity can possibly or logically be omniscient.' A better and simpler way of logically proving that omniscience is impossible is available through using the conundrum of the possibility of 'limited intelligence' which it is logically impossible to overcome (it being a negative that one cannot possibly disprove). The conundrum and logical proof here is, 'Nothing can be sure of not being limited in intelligence (or knowledge) because limited intelligence might include (even for a potential God) inability to see one's own limited intelligence.' Obviously it is evident, self-evident and undeniable as a logical possibility that inability to see one's own limited intelligence might be a consequence of being limited in intelligence or knowledge. Given that that is possible, which cannot logically be denied because it cannot be proved that that is ever impossible as a possibility, how can any entity actually know for certain that it is not in that situation? Bear in mind that if it were in that situation it would not know it anyhow. There can be no unambiguous distinguishing mark for any entity between its being limited in knowledge and its being unlimited in knowledge if it already is apparently unique and seemingly has no limitations to its knowledge. Thus a possibility that cannot properly be logically discounted is presented even to it (a potentially omniscient entity) and its inability to discount that possibility means that it cannot be omniscient. Indeed since nothing that is possibly otherwise omniscient can overcome that hurdle, this point shows that nothing is omniscient and nothing can be omniscient. So by that means it can be established that omniscience is impossible. Therefore as nothing can be omniscient the second premise of the logical disproof of God's existence is therefore definitely established.

So both premises of the logical deduction are safely established and the conclusion that is deduced from the two premises follows with inexorable and correct logic from those premises. Therefore the application of logic in my disproof of the existence of God is not flawed. So, Logic having been validly applied, my argument is invulnerable to any objection concerning its use of Logic.

(v) The Argument Is Of No Practical Consequence

The possible objection here is that this disproof of the existence of God is purely theoretical and can be of no practical consequence.

In the sense that it is possible that something, be it a powerful daemon or be it a self-deluded entity, mistakenly believing itself to be God (and even if God cannot exist, of course it is possible for some entities still to actually believe that they are God) may punish us humans terribly for failing to believe in 'God', my argument may indeed be academic. A sufficiently powerful entity may of course still terrorise human beings. Naturally so far as human beings are concerned it is really an academic point whether they are in fact to be terrorised by a genuine God or by a mere daemon! So obviously practical power is still practical power and so long as that power lasts it is in a practical sense completely academic whether that power is underpinned by a justifiable certainty in its status or is ultimately uncertain. It is even academic whether the exerciser of power could even be bothered about the academic or existential status of his power!

Yet this consideration cannot properly negate this argument because while power may be at least partly a practical concept, God is an intellectual concept. The status and permanence of an entity's attributes are essential in the identification, even self-identification, of God and in the distinction between a genuine monotheistic God and a daemon. So if the term God is to have a significant meaning at all, the underlying and indeed intellectual basis of God's qualities must be critical. It is true that there may at a given time and at a given space appear to be no practical difference to the unpowerful observer (such as us humans) between a particularly powerful daemon and God. However it would be wrong to believe that such a daemon necessarily has a comprehensive extension of power along all directions in both Space and Time (such as an existent God would have to have). Whether a powerful daemon exists is an entirely empirical question, but whether a monotheistic God can exist and be identified is necessarily at least partially a theoretical, philosophical question.

However we are concerned in this book with the possible existence or non-existence of God and not with the existence or non-existence of powerful daemons. So this objection (even though true!) that it may possibly make no practical difference to us whether God actually exists is irrelevant to arguments (including this argument) against the actual existence of God.

(vi) God Has Maximal Not Absolute Knowledge

I suppose theists might well try the same manoeuvre in respect to knowledge as they have often done in respect to power when they hit theoretical problems with 'omnipotence'. Theists tend to claim that in reality God is not literally omnipotent but rather possesses the maximum power that is logically achievable. Likewise they might claim (by way of objection to my argument) God is not quite literally omniscient but rather possesses the maximum possible logically achievable knowledge. So they might claim God really has (and needs to have) only maximal knowledge even within the context of a theoretical universal uncertainty.

However there is a difference between the concept of maximal power and a possible concept of maximal knowledge that is fundamental. I admit I am personally not really happy with the downgrading of divine omnipotence into divine maximal power. (I think it rather contravenes proper trading standards practice to describe God as all-powerful, omnipotent and able to do anything, in a word extraordinary, but deliver an inferior God product that contrary to the tenor of the propaganda can only do the relatively ordinary that other things, any daemon, given sufficient power, can do.) Yet I acknowledge that 'maximal power' is a viable concept. Maximal power means that God cannot accomplish what is contrary to Logic (such as creating a square circle), but that does not detract from nor alter God's ability to accomplish all logically possible things. God's edifice of practical power would remain intact. By contrast the result would be very different if one were to whittle down God's knowledge from omniscience to maximal knowledge. The inability of a God to accomplish the logically impossible does not in any way undermine the edifice of God's ability to accomplish the logically possible. By contrast the inability of God to possess ultimate certainty must undermine all God's supposed knowledge and indeed threaten to bring the whole edifice of his supposed knowledge crashing down.

This is because if things can be – as they surely can be – put into another and different focus in the light of greater knowledge, all so called previous knowledge may have to be reassessed and found to be not only incomplete but sometimes fundamentally wrong. This is akin to the difference between Science (like knowledge) and Technology (like power). If new technological inventions like the motor car are produced existing inventions like the train are still valid technologically. By contrast if a new scientific theory is adopted such as for instance evolution or relativity the whole edifice of existing scientific so-called knowledge in that area is undermined and altered. So in the absence of total knowledge that cannot even potentially be swept away by further discoveries, maximal knowledge is inadequate because it cannot erect an edifice of relevant knowledge that is definitely sustainable come what may. A similar consideration also applies if it is logically impossible to be absolutely certain of predicting the future sequence of events correctly. If things are liable (at least eventually) to change radically and decisively, yet unpredictably in the future, then even what may seem to be divine now may be reduced to rubble in the changed circumstances of the future.

So my disproof of the existence of God cannot be rebutted by a qualification or downgrading of God's knowledge from 'omniscience' to a concept akin to 'maximal knowledge'. Short of total knowledge which entails a certainty of knowledge that it is logically impossible to achieve, there is no lesser amount of knowledge that can render one invulnerable to being overcome by outside forces from a realm beyond one's own knowledge. Therefore this sort of objection to my disproof of God's existence is not valid and cannot properly be sustained.

So I have examined all six of the types of objection to my disproof of the existence of God that I can presently conceive might with even any superficial degree of credibility be put forward. As I have shown them all to be either invalid or ineffective against my disproof of the existence of God, I cannot see that any possible objection to my argument is likely even to unsettle my argument. It seems invulnerable to all possible objections.

Of course if the logic of the disproof of the existence of God is correct and complete, then logically there can be no valid objection to the argument. However looking for but finding upon consideration no valid objection to the argument in its way (though admittedly not in an entirely satisfactory nor foolproof way) confirms that the logic of the argument is likely to be correct. Put another way if an objection had been found to be effective then either that objection would not have been rebutted properly or the argument itself must have some unseen logical defect. Fortunately however this seems not to be the case.

So these possible attempts to undermine the argument by such objections fail. The argument that disproves the existence of God through the logical impossibility of anything, including an otherwise potential God, being omniscient emerges as strong and as valid as when originally stated and logically demonstrated.

E. The Argument In Perspective

I have set before you a logical disproof of the existence of God. The disproof is absolute. It even applies if contrary to expectations Logic cannot be relied upon throughout the whole Universe. The standard of this proof is not merely a proof beyond reasonable doubt, it is at least a proof beyond conceivable doubt. No sustainable scenario can be constructed in which my proof does not apply. There is no conceivable way in which any entity can be justifiably absolutely certain beyond doubt that it is genuinely God. So no entity can be God because certain knowledge that no greater force than it exists anywhere at all is essential to it being God (at least a monotheistic God). So there can be no God.

In the end it is the very supreme qualities necessarily hypothecated of God that have in this argument proved to be the Achilles' heel of the God concept. God's supposed and indeed essential unique and supreme qualities have proved to be the undoing of the God concept since it can be shown that at least one of these unique yet necessary qualities – omniscience – is absolutely unattainable. The very notion that gives the concept of God much of its theoretical power and grandiosity – its unique omniscience – is also a means by which it is being proved that God cannot exist. Omniscience is essential to a monotheistic God because in the absence of omniscience it cannot be sure that there is not some yet greater entity somewhere above even it and capable of destroying it. Yet omniscience is a quality which is proved to be unattainable which means that nothing can have that quality and nothing can therefore be God. Of course if God could have made do with a less supreme quality, merely immense knowledge, it would have been impossible to disprove that some entity superior, perhaps unimaginably superior, to us humans could possess immense knowledge – and therefore such a disproof would not have worked. However immense knowledge is not sufficient for a monotheistic God because it leaves open the possibility that somewhere somehow in an area even beyond its immense understanding a yet greater entity exists. Such a greater entity may then be lurking around and be ready in its own good time to dislodge our hypothetical God from its divine pedestal. Nor would even immense knowledge be enough knowledge to ensure a potential God can have absolute reassurance that it is indeed genuinely immortal, omnipresent, omnipotent and ultimately consciously controlling. So, ironically, a monotheistic God that has been exalted by his assumed unique and supreme qualities is also being destroyed as a concept when it is shown that some of these same supreme qualities are incapable of being confirmed in practice. So such qualities are therefore themselves reasons why God can be proved not to actually exist.

Now that God has been shown to be a logically impossible concept and so incapable of existing, belief in God and even faith in God's existence are also revealed to be plain wrong. It is feasible to have a belief or a faith in what is still a possibility (even an unlikely possibility such as aliens from outer space landing on Earth within one's lifetime) but when a notion has been disproved, it is no longer a matter for belief or faith but a matter of being correct or incorrect. On this (correct) basis there is no longer any scope for belief or faith in the existence of God. It has been proved to be incorrect (i.e. wrong) to be a monotheist and correct (i.e. right) to be an atheist. By analogy once upon a time several thousand years ago (and arguably even several hundred years ago) it was a fair matter for conjecture or belief or even faith whether the Earth is flat or spherical. However now with our greater knowledge it has become a matter of being right or wrong, wrong to believe the Earth is flat and right to believe that the Earth is spherical. In practice what has happened is that after overwhelming scientific evidence appeared that the Earth is spherical people subsequently for the most part came to accept that in consequence of such evidence the Earth is spherical. Eventually after some time only a very few people have persisted in the view that the Earth is flat. Of course the existence or non-existence of God is a greater and more fundamental and more emotive issue for people than the shape of the Earth. Of course the disproof of God's existence is more theoretically based than knowledge of the shape of the Earth is (at least with present technology). Of course people are very often inclined to be irrational rather than logical. Nevertheless I suspect that in the end as with the shape of the Earth peoples' beliefs will eventually follow theoretical knowledge. After the logical proof that God cannot exist, people subsequently for the most part will come to accept that in consequence of such proof God cannot exist. Eventually after some time only a very small minority of people may still persist in the view that God exists. So in time the Gods of Judaism, Christianity, Islam and Sikhism and many more besides will fall into the dustbin (or annals) of history just as formerly the Gods of Greece, Rome, Carthage and the Norsemen did! However that is speculation and is subject to the sometimes irrational vagaries of human nature. What is beyond doubt is that I have now provided absolute and indubitable disproof of the existence of a monotheistic God which no objection can overcome. Therefore like it or not, make of it what you will, monotheism is wrong and atheism is right!

CHAPTER 6

The 'Some Of God's Defining Qualities Cannot Exist' Argument

A. Prologue

Like some of the other arguments in this book, the approach of this argument is not absolutely new but this argument constitutes a refinement, extension and improvement of an existing, albeit nowadays unfashionable line of argument. In particular there has historically been much dispute over whether a potential God can possibly be truly omnipotent. However this argument does not as yet seem to have extended to any substantial consideration of whether a potential God can possibly be omniscient, supremely good and our purpose giver. Nevertheless I am going to look at this argument in the context of all God's essential defining qualities – qualities which are essentially defining for a potential God and not merely attributes that happen to be associated with God. So I submit a major improvement to this argument is the extension of this argument from being just about God's omnipotence to being far more comprehensive and relating to God's other defining qualities (such as 'purpose giver' as well). The argument over whether God is precluded from existing because of the apparent impossibility of being truly omnipotent was once quite common and was evidently actively considered many hundreds of years ago. However that discussion eventually withered and fell out of fashion. Perhaps the compromise solution to the argument eventually became the intellectual consensus which was adopted by most people, including most major Christian theologians (such as Thomas Aquinas and William of Occam). The compromise consensus was the view that in reality in the last resort God is not actually absolutely omnipotent but merely 'maximally powerful' (i.e.

as powerful as an entity can possibly be within the parameters of Logic). By widening the argument beyond the one quality of omnipotence to other qualities absolutely essential to a possible God, I believe I have overcome the manoeuvre of 'maximal power' which has up to now been widely seen as the solution to this line of argument.

However to return to the beginning of this argument, let us look briefly at the historical development so far of argumentation about the possibility or impossibility of God's essential qualities existing. It is not known when this argument originated. However we do know the limitations of polytheistic Gods (who were often deemed to be subject to Fate) had been an ancient subject for consideration. Quite probably consideration of the limitations of the powers of polytheistic Gods naturally sparked considerations of the limitations of the power of a monotheistic God when the concept of monotheism developed. Certainly Pliny The Elder (23-79 AD), an ancient Roman, was living in an age which was dominated by polytheism when he considered this matter and wrote (in his Natural History – Book II v27) as follows – 'But the chief consolations for nature's imperfection in the case of man are that not even for God are all things possible – for he cannot... cause a man that has lived not to have lived or one that has held high office not to have held it – and he has no power over what is past save to forget it, and he cannot cause twice ten not to be twenty or do many things on similar lines: which facts unquestionably demonstrate the power of nature, and prove that it is that we mean by the word 'God'.' Pliny's conclusion that God is merely in reality another word for Nature is nowadays acceptable to neither theists nor atheists. Yet one can sympathise with Pliny in finding that an ideal way to reconcile the existence of God with the evidently great power of nature over seemingly all things. Thereafter in the mediaeval world there must, one can surely surmise, have been some objections raised about the logic of the practical existence of God's essential qualities, at least his omnipotence. It was much discussed by Thomas Aquinas (c1225-1274), William of Occam (c1285-1349), Peter Damian (c1007-1072) and others, usually to modify the doctrine of divine omnipotence so as to reconcile it with Logic, yet keeping as much of divine omnipotence as possible within the bounds of Logic. A certain amount of debate on this has continued down the ages – just a few like Martin Luther (1483-1546) claimed God can do 'absolutely everything'. Quite commonly God's essential characteristics including omnipotence came to be listed both by theists like René Descartes (1596-1650) and by non-theists such as Charles Bradlaugh (1833-1891). In more modern times some debate has still continued. The arguments have been refined by some – John Mackie asked, 'Can an omnipotent being make things he cannot control?' And contemporary theologians like Alvin Platinga have attempted to further refine definitions of God's omnipotence into such concepts as 'maximal power' to take account of Logic. Still the more general – and I think more intractable – logical problems concerning some of God's other essential qualities are neglected. Here I am trying to remedy that. I also think what makes the concept of a monotheistic God particularly vulnerable to absolute disproof (far more so than the less absolute polytheistic Gods or demi-Gods as in Hinduism) is the sheer absolutism of God's essential qualities: I hope that comes to be realised.

I turn to considering God's various qualities so as to evaluate them in terms of whether their existence is even theoretically possible, let alone actually realised in a monotheistic God. The qualities to be considered are inevitably those qualities that are God's essential defining qualities. I listed, and listed with good reason, in the Introduction to this book eight such qualities. It is just conceivable – though I would resist it – that upon analysis one might subtract one or two qualities from that list. It is rather more likely that one should add one or two qualities which I have either overlooked or discounted to that list. However it is from the list of God's essential defining qualities that one should start in arguing the case that God's essential defining qualities cannot exist. The eight essential defining qualities a potential monotheistic God must have in my view are that he must be 'eternal, omnipresent, consciously controlling, our ultimate creator, omnipotent, supremely good, omniscient and our purpose giver'. We will have to look at these qualities individually to try to separate them out into two categories. In the first category are those qualities which in theoretical terms are not inherently incapable of existence (even if in fact they may not actually exist in practice). In the second category are those qualities which are even theoretically incapable of existence and so are really absolutely impossible of realisation by anybody or anything, even by a potential God.

Quite clearly some of these eight qualities are not, so far as at least we humans are aware, absolutely theoretically impossible in terms of existence. Their existence might indeed seem highly improbable but in the case of some qualities it is not so far as we know inherently absolutely impossible. It is not theoretically absolutely impossible so far as I can see that an entity should be 'eternal'. It is also certainly theoretically possible for an entity to be consciously controlling and exercise control over us and theoretically at least (so far as I can see) over the whole Universe. Nor would I claim that it is absolutely impossible for an entity to be 'omnipresent' with the qualification that I am not particularly happy with the very concept of omnipresence anyhow. (I suppose 'omnipresence' might range from knowledge of what is going on everywhere which is O.K. by me as a concept to a sort of permeating physical presence everywhere which I am not at all happy with.) A fourth quality which I personally would concede is not inherently absolutely impossible is that of being 'our ultimate creator'. (I suppose 'our ultimate creator' as a concept must be the uncreated entity that originated the 'creation' process in the Universe out of which we humans came either directly or indirectly to exist.)

So I concede it may not be inherently absolutely impossible for some entity to have four of these qualities – 'eternal, omnipresent, consciously controlling and our ultimate creator'. (I assume here that 'omnipresence' is a possible viable quality which I admit is doubtful – however I suppose if it is not viable anyhow 'God' may well be able to do without it!) However I cannot see that any particular entity could possibly know for certain that he has any, let alone all four of these qualities. How can any entity possibly know that it is actually eternal and will live through all the future before the future has occurred? How can any entity possibly know for sure that there are not regions somewhere beyond its apparent 'omnipresence'? How can any entity possibly know for sure that it is actually 'consciously controlling' rather than being merely 'apparently controlling' or is itself not somehow being 'controlled' unbeknown to it itself? How can any entity know for sure that it is the 'ultimate creator' and has not unbeknown to it somehow ultimately itself been created? So

while I am willing to concede that these four attributes of a
monotheistic God are not theoretically speaking inherently
impossible, I think that definite knowledge of them existing in any
particular individual entity is logically inherently impossible.
However this particular argument is not that God's essential defining
characteristics cannot be identified in any particular entity (which I
argued elsewhere) but that God's essential defining characteristics
inherently cannot actually exist. So with those caveats I do concede
that the four qualities of being 'eternal, omnipresent, consciously
controlling and our ultimate creator' may at least theoretically, albeit
improbably, exist. Therefore to develop this argument I must turn
my attention to a monotheistic God's other four defining essential
characteristics – omnipotence, supreme goodness, omniscience and
being our purpose giver.

I turn therefore to 'omnipotence'. As previously stated this is the
one quality essential to God about which there has already been
much discussion and controversy. I think a fair conclusion from that
discussion with which even most theologians would agree is that if
'omnipotence' is taken to mean absolute omnipotence by which God
is capable of doing absolutely everything even God cannot be
omnipotent. It is absurd to claim that it is even possible to create
'a square circle' or 'to have power over what is past except to forget
it or obliterate or change memories of it'. Even apart from what is
logically impossible it could hardly be feasible for a monotheistic
God to create an object he cannot lift or create an entity more
powerful than itself! So despite occasional objections to the
contrary it is generally accepted that there are some things that
cannot possibly be done even with the greatest conceivable amount
of power at one's command. So it is therefore generally accepted that
even God cannot accomplish such things. So where does that leave
the concept of God's omnipotence? Well, I believe one has two
choices. Either one may argue over whether nothing can be
absolutely omnipotent in which case one might argue God cannot
exist. Or one may consider toning down the concept of
'omnipotence' to 'the greatest logically achievable power' or
'maximal power' and attach that 'maximal power' instead of 'absolute
power' to a monotheistic God and claim that is all a monotheistic
God really needs to have. Not surprisingly most theologians through

the ages (from at least mediaeval times) have chosen to tone down or redefine the concept of 'omnipotence' rather than succumb to Logic in an intellectual tussle over the very viability of the concept of God. But is the manoeuvre of toning down or redefining omnipotence to accommodate a possible God really legitimate? Certainly it is a major concession to Logic even among religious faiths to bring their God within the domain of Logic, so foregoing any claim that even a monotheistic God can do the logically impossible or by implication exist beyond the parameters of rationality and Logic. I acknowledge that concession here from most theologians that God can only exist within the bounds of the logically possible. I also acknowledge that redrawing the boundary of omnipotence from absolute omnipotence to the maximum degree of omnipotence that is logically possible does not in practice undermine the edifice on which the whole concept of God is built. I accept this proposed alternative boundary of 'maximal power' is a completely defensible boundary and does not undermine the concept or possible viability of God in other respects. Therefore in these circumstances on balance I myself am willing to accept in the instance of omnipotence that 'omnipotence' in relation to God can probably be legitimately redefined. So I am willing to accept the concept of God's omnipotence can be changed from its probable (or commonest) original scriptural and religious meaning of 'absolutely all-powerful' to mean 'maximally powerful within the parameters of Logic'. I know that in allowing this redefinition of God's omnipotence I am depriving myself of the possibility of a simple disproof of God's existence as follows: - 'God is defined to be and necessarily claims to be (absolutely) omnipotent. Yet as several examples (such as not being able to create a square circle or in the case of God an entity more powerful than itself) show, no entity can be absolutely omnipotent. Therefore God cannot exist, as he must lack at least one of the qualities essential to being God, namely omnipotence.' However I am myself as a concession generously prepared to accept the proposed redefinition of omnipotence to suit the concept of a monotheistic God because it does not in practice undermine the foundations of the concept of even a monotheistic God or its possible effects upon humans or any other entity. Yet I do still note that a redefinition of the term 'omnipotence' has been found to be necessary to avoid the destruction of the concept of a monotheistic God by the theoretical impossibility of any entity being absolutely omnipotent. I also note with satisfaction that even most of the most distinguished theologians (such as Thomas Aquinas) have effectively acknowledged that in a clash between the supremacy of God and the supremacy of logical reality (as happened over the question of 'absolute omnipotence') the concept of God has backed down and logical reality has won out. I will presently be claiming that in respect of some of God's other essential qualities it is not going to be possible for the concept of God to be revised adequately to reconcile itself with logical reality. In these instances the concept of God which is here acknowledged to be subordinate to logical reality cannot in fact survive the unavoidable conflict between monotheism and logical reality that a thorough analysis of the concept of a monotheistic God and of logical reality will reveal. So in the end even though it may escape in respect of 'omnipotence', monotheism will be completely destroyed as a viable concept by the force of logical reality.

Having reached an accommodation in relation to the possible existence of 'omnipotence' by allowing it to be redefined as 'maximal power' let us examine the concept of 'supreme goodness' in relation to a possible God. The argument here is roughly this:-

a) God must be supremely good, otherwise he would not be God.

b) Nothing can be supremely good because there is no objective standard of supreme goodness.

c) Therefore as no entity can be supremely good, God cannot exist.

It is normally assumed in monotheism that God is supremely good and that supreme goodness is one of God's necessary qualities. That assumption is justifiable because it is really the dimension of supreme goodness that most distinguishes 'God' from 'a supremely powerful daemon' and makes God however powerful he may be the legitimate object of voluntary and respectable human worship and religion. Without that quality of supreme goodness 'God' would lose his moral and respect-deserving dimension and would be merely a daemon that is a political or astronomical feature of the Universe. So monotheistic religions accordingly do emphasise God's supreme goodness.

However the notion of 'supreme or ultimate goodness' tends to be assumed among humans rather than examined closely. Yet this apparently clear notion of supreme goodness which seems so obvious to humans when talked about at a distance does, I submit, fall quite apart becoming first confused and then untenable upon close examination. I suspect humans have an instinctive, human-based notion of goodness, just as women usually have an instinctive notion of parenting. So the human perspective is in many matters not neutral nor objective but weighted towards some subjective, albeit widely held human opinion. A good example of this is in respect to 'beauty' which is not absolute but reflects subjective human notions. I think in the same way any notion of goodness or supreme goodness (except where 'good' signifies 'efficient' means to accomplish a designated end) is a subjective notion rather than an objective and absolute notion and therefore nothing is in objective terms supremely good. I hope others might agree with this but even if they don't I can sustain my point that there is no objective supreme goodness in another even clearer way. This arises from an ambiguity in the meaning of 'goodness', an ambiguity which is actually found in religion. 'Goodness' when analysed relates to two different concepts, not just one concept. 'Goodness' can mean 'benevolent' or it can mean 'just'. So 'supreme goodness' may mean being 'supremely benevolent and merciful' to everyone, even to conscious wrong-doers or it can mean being 'supremely fair and just' to everyone, giving everyone their just deserts. Of course any judge should know the results of benevolence and pure justice are very different, the one resulting in mercy to criminals, the other resulting in proportionate punishment. There is no objective nor agreed way of determining whether supreme goodness consists of supreme benevolence or supreme fairness (or justice). In the absence of any such agreed determination, goodness and supreme goodness are merely vague and ultimately ambiguous terms that cannot properly exist in objective and absolute form.

The conclusion here follows logically from the premises. Since no entity can be supremely good, the entity, God, that must be supremely good in order to exist cannot exist. I suppose when one reaches that conclusion, one should re-examine the premises of the argument. The first premise that God must be supremely good, otherwise he would not be God is a necessity for making the concept of God significant in a moral and religious way. Accordingly monotheistic religions do now insist that God is not merely a tutelary polytheistic deity (indeed as he is in monotheism all-powerful there is nothing beyond himself for him to guard against) but is primarily a paragon God, being a paragon not merely of power but also of virtue and goodness. So if for whatever reason a potential God is not or cannot be supreme in goodness, that God must inevitably be reduced in status from God to a mere supremely powerful daemon. Therefore the first premise must be correct in relation to God. The second premise – that nothing can be supremely good because there is no objective standard of supreme goodness – is also on the face of it unassailable. However could this problem in future be overcome for 'God' by redefining 'supreme goodness' just as in the past theologians have managed to redefine 'omnipotence'? I don't know except that it cannot be done without overcoming enormous difficulties. 'God' is of course associated both with traditions of justice and also benevolence and so it would be difficult to plump for one rather than the other and any proportion such as two thirds 'just' and one third 'benevolent' would be arbitrary. Furthermore both justice and benevolence are to an extent subjective concepts and the evidence of this world also suggests that 'God' is neither exceedingly just nor exceedingly benevolent! So I do not know (though I rather doubt it) whether 'supreme goodness' can be legitimately redefined to make it into a coherent, appropriate and theoretically possible concept. However I do know that if 'supreme goodness' is not so redefined God can be shown not to exist because God's essential defining quality of 'supreme goodness' is inherently subjective and also muddled (as between justice and benevolence) and so is incapable of ever even theoretically achieving real existence!

So with that unsatisfactory conclusion to the quality of 'supreme goodness' leaving it in the air awaiting either destruction or an attempt at redefinition to avoid destruction that may or may not be successful, let us turn our attention to the quality of 'omniscience'. I contend that it is impossible for 'God' or anything else to be omniscient and the argument is as follows:

a) God must be omniscient, otherwise he would not be God.

b) It is impossible for any entity to be sure of being omniscient.

(If one cannot be sure of one's own omniscience, one cannot therefore be omniscient.)

c) Therefore as no entity can be omniscient, God cannot exist.

This is an argument I have developed more fully in The Universal Uncertainty Argument. So I will deal relatively briefly with 'omniscience' here. Omniscience is necessarily one of God's essential qualities and this must be so because knowledge is ultimately interconnected. One cannot be sure of anything much in relation to one's place in the Universe unless one is sure of everything. One cannot be sure one is the most powerful or the ultimately creative entity unless one knows all about all entities. One cannot even be certain one will survive until tomorrow. Nor can it be that God need not be omniscient because without omniscience over all things 'God' could not be certain of being able to exercise power, especially future power, over all things. Then even 'God', let alone us, could not know that he is genuinely 'God' – an absurd situation! The second premise of this argument, that omniscience is impossible for any entity holds true because there is no verifiable route, no technique for attaining omniscience over all things. One can never know that some more powerful force, or thing that can change everything all of a sudden, does not lie beyond one's ability to see it. One can never be sure, especially if one is as unique as 'God' would inevitably have to be, that one might (even if one has lived through past eternity) not drop dead suddenly and unaccountably tomorrow. Clearly if the two premises, first that God would have to be omniscient, and second that omniscience is impossible for any entity, both hold true it logically follows that God cannot exist. Even if one were to claim that God might exist beyond all logic then neither the supposed God nor us have any way of being certain of that proposition – and so to all intents and purposes even upon that supposition God lacks omniscience (or indeed in the absence of Logic lacks any really reliable knowledge at all) and so effectively does not exist. Nor is the concept of 'maximal omniscience' feasible because knowledge in the Universe is like a jigsaw and without omniscience the whole picture of the jigsaw (Universe) is uncertain. A deficiency in omniscience therefore undermines the whole structure of one's knowledge.

So there seems to be no way out of this argument. Omniscience is both a necessary quality for a monotheistic God and at the same time a quality that no entity can possibly possess – these points combine to prove that God cannot exist. So this is an effective and decisive form of the argument that God cannot exist because some of God's qualities cannot exist. Indeed the argument in relation to omniscience is probably the most effective and unchallengeable of all the arguments about God not being able to exist because one or other of his defining qualities cannot exist in any entity.

Nevertheless I will henceforth (after this Prologue) consider primarily though not quite exclusively the essential quality of God being 'our purpose giver' in relation to this argument, that God cannot exist because some of God's defining qualities cannot exist. Meanwhile to summarise so far, I have discounted four of my list (namely being 'eternal, omnipresent, consciously controlling and our ultimate creator') of God's eight essential qualities for the purposes of proving that they are impossible qualities for any entity even in purely hypothetical, theoretical terms to hold. Of the remaining four qualities I have argued in relation of 'omnipotence' and 'supreme goodness' that as they naturally stand they cannot be even theoretically attained by any entity and so 'God' cannot have such qualities – but with an amount of refining and redefining it may be possible for an entity to attain those sorts of qualities albeit in a more modest or less confused form. Concerning the quality of 'omniscience' I have shown it is necessarily impossible for any entity, even a potential God, to have it. I am soon going to consider the quality of being 'our purpose giver' with a view to demonstrating that it too is a quality essential to a monotheistic God which it is impossible for any entity, even a potential God, to attain.

B. Summary Of The Argument

1. God must have certain characteristic qualities (such as providing purpose to life), otherwise he would not be God.

2. But it is impossible for any entity to possess some of these qualities (such as providing purpose to life since we can find no real purpose and therefore we in practice have no ultimate purpose to our lives) that are essential to God.

3. Therefore since some of God's essential qualities (such as being the purpose provider to life) cannot possibly exist in any entity, God cannot exist.

C. Explaining The Argument

I will first explain this argument in general terms and then I will go through it with specific reference to the characteristic of 'our purpose giver' that a potential god requires.

If God exists he must have certain qualities, essential qualities or characteristics that mark him out as God and distinguish him from entities that are not God. In the absence of such qualities he could not properly be called God, at least a monotheistic God and he would not correspond with the God concept of the various monotheistic religions. These qualities have been listed by various authors and though they may vary somewhat between authoritative commentators they always should include characteristics such as omnipotence, omniscience, immortality, supreme goodness and being the endower of purpose to the Universe. It is for instance impossible to have a monotheistic God who is not eternal (that might die tomorrow or might already have died), that is not supremely good (otherwise why worship God, if one is not forced to do so?) and that does not infuse purpose into existence (otherwise why bother at all if our existence does not matter whatever we do?).

So having established that God must have some essential characteristics, the object of this argument is to show that it is impossible for any entity to have one or more of those characteristics essential to God. The demonstration of this may come in terms of sheer logic (as with omnipotence) or the nature of existence (omniscience) or irreconcilability with our existence and the world as we know it (as with supreme goodness and purpose).

Once it has been shown that it is impossible for any entity to possess some characteristic that is essential to God, then it has been shown that God cannot exist. If some quality (be it 'omnipotence', 'omniscience', 'supreme goodness' or 'purpose giver') essential to God's very existence must be lacking in all entities, it therefore must be lacking in any entity that might otherwise be God. Therefore God could not logically exist. Therefore God does not exist. And so the existence of God has been disproved if this line of argument is correct.

So that is the general theory of this type of argument against the existence of God. Now I will turn to its specific application in relation to God's quality of being the purpose giver to life.

It is surely an essential quality of God that he gives purpose to life. It is essential that there be purpose to life if any of God's other supposed qualities are ultimately to matter. Otherwise it is an academic and ultimately meaningless thing whether or not an omnipotent, eternal, omniscient entity exists or not. Indeed it is then even academic whether we have been created or not and whether we live or not! So purpose is needed to consummate God's other qualities such as being our creator, controlling the world, being eternal and possibly even as part of being supremely good. At the very least one may say even if a God-like entity, a great daemon existed, why have religion if there is ultimately no purpose to it all? Without purpose our world would merely be a mammoth structure or folly without foundations and without anything to bind it all together and make it meaningful. So overall purpose is urgently needed, indeed it is essential. It is clearly the responsibility of any monotheistic God as the supposed ultimate creator of the Universe to ultimately endow that purpose (or at any rate ensure that purpose is endowed) to the Universe. Endowing purpose to the Universe is therefore just as much a function and just as essential a function of a monotheistic God as is ultimately creating the Universe in the first place. So the first premise, which is that 'God' must ultimately provide purpose to life, otherwise he would not be God, is clearly correct.

The second premise of this particular form of the argument concerning purpose is that there is and can be no ultimate purpose to our lives. When confronted with the question what is the purpose to life, the popular theistic answer is 'to worship God'. However to non-theists God's very existence, let alone his narcissism through his creation, is not apparent, nor indeed is the purpose of a purpose like worshipping God. Yet what is apparent is the circularity of their argument which answers questions about God's creative actions only in terms of God. (This flawed circularity is for instance evident if one asks what is the purpose of life, is told 'to worship' God and then asks what is the purpose worshipping God to be told 'to fulfil one's purpose in life'.) For the rest I personally have never heard an alternative version of the purpose of life (which God supposedly created) proffered by orthodox monotheists, or indeed an ultimate purpose to life that can withstand genuine examination proffered by anybody. I venture to state that there is no ultimate purpose to life. (I personally see life as a subjectively interesting but ultimately purposeless journey from birth to death. If anything at all – which is doubtful – the purpose, which is artificial, would lie in the journey or the living but that can exist independently of God and that is evidently not even a conscious purpose for people!) At any rate no purpose to life is readily apparent to us humans who are living life. As we know of no purpose to life, a purpose to life might as well not exist so far as we are concerned because we cannot then consciously be fulfilling that purpose, nor even living our lives in the knowledge of that or any purpose! So the second premise of this argument, that there is no ultimate purpose to our lives, is upon close examination clearly correct.

The conclusion of this particular argument follows logically from its two premises. Furthermore this argument concerning purpose to one's existence cannot be evaded in a similar way to the way in which the argument concerning omnipotence (or even supreme goodness) may perhaps be evaded. There is either an ultimate purpose to life or there is not an ultimate purpose to life. There cannot be degrees of purpose so ambiguity and questions of 'maximal purpose' are out of the question here. Nor do I find great linguistic difficulties with the concept of purpose. So this argument constitutes a strong and valid argument against the existence of God. It is surely an essential characteristic of an existent monotheistic God to provide an ultimate purpose to life and to the whole 'created' system. Yet no genuine ultimate purpose can be found to life by those who should know of any purpose, namely those who are consciously living life. Therefore it is apparent that God does not exist – or at the very least God himself (if you would even call a powerful daemon who cannot endow purpose to his creation God) does not therefore ultimately matter! (Isn't a 'God' that is not ultimately significant or does not ultimately matter a contradiction in terms?)

D. Possible Objections To The Argument

I shall now consider various possible objections to this argument against the existence of God based upon the impossibility of some of God's essential defining characteristics existing even theoretically in the Universe. I will refer particularly to the non-existence of ultimate purpose to either the Universe or indeed to our own individual lives.

(i) We Are Presumptuous In Believing We Can Define God (Human Knowledge Being Limited)

The objection here is that we being human and finite should not even presume to define an infinite God. Nor should we humans according to this objection presume to attribute qualities to God.

This objection is superficially attractive but is flawed when examined in more detail. In the first place it ill behoves anybody to proclaim both that God exists and also that God's characteristics cannot be understood. If God's characteristics cannot be understood by us, how then can we presume to know, as monotheists claim to know, that God actually exists? This is an instance of the theistic comprehension paradox – 'I do not know what God is like (or what qualities God has). Yet I know that God exists'. To know that God exists, or even to believe that God exists implies a knowledge of at least some characteristics by which God can be known! Indeed without such a knowledge of some of God's characteristics one cannot legitimately recognise nor believe in God.

The second flaw to this objection is that this argument is not really claiming to define God comprehensively nor to define the way in which God works. It merely identifies some characteristic qualities that would have to be essential to an existent God, qualities without which an entity would not be able to amount to a monotheistic God! For instance whatever else God may or may not be, he must be eternal (or always existing) – otherwise he would not be God. A God that may die tomorrow, or indeed may already have died is not possible as a monotheistic God because if God may be mortal most of God's other essential qualities cannot be guaranteed to continue to exist into the future. Indeed in that case God would then be subordinate to his own fate, to his own mortality. We may pray to God for a long life for ourselves, but we can hardly pray for a long life for God – and in any event to whom should we then pray? Likewise God must clearly have certain other characteristics if he is to exist as God. Another characteristic quality God must have is supreme power (or omnipotence) – otherwise we would have the absurd and inherently contradictory position whereby God might be able to accomplish less than some other entity and may even be subject in some ways to the power of some other entity! Another characteristic quality God must have is that he must be the endower of purpose to the whole Universe – otherwise the whole Universe (which God supposedly created) would ultimately be meaningless. Then God too (if he could even be said to exist in a purposeless Universe) would be merely an incidental and unmeaningful fact of nature, amounting ultimately to inconsequential trivia, albeit on a grand scale! So in essence though this objection concerning our defining God may properly caution us against defining God too precisely, there are some minimal presumptions that effectively form part of a definition of a meaningful, religious, monotheistic God which we can and should legitimately make about God (should God exist).

The third point here is that the attribution of qualities to God is in reality common ground between practically all theists and atheists anyhow – it is not some remarkable assumption only I or indeed only a few people have made. Even in the Bible God has certainly got absolutist qualities, particularly omnipotence ascribed to him – for instance, 'I know that you (God) are all-powerful' (Job 42.2). Among both theistic philosophers such as René Descartes (1596-1650) and atheistic thinkers such as Charles Bradlaugh (1833-1891) qualities such as immortality, omnipotence and omniscience are considered integral to the concept of God. Even those philosophers such as Diogenes the Areopagite (fl. c500AD) and Moses Maimonides who have been most reluctant to allow that God can be described through positive qualities settled for a negative means of description (the 'via negativa'). They described God by what he is not, such as not mortal which I think in the end amounts to much the same as positive attributes such as immortal. At any rate they allowed, as all theologians and all who believe in God must practically inevitably allow, that something descriptive concerning God's qualities can be known about God.

So, to conclude, there is no logical substance in the objection that we are being overly presumptuous in claiming to know what some of God's qualities must be. We would of course be excessively presumptuous if we claimed to know everything about God or to know all of God's characteristics. But we can at least know what qualities are essential to God inasmuch as he would be deficient as God and therefore not be God if he were to lack such qualities.

(ii) Is Ultimate Purpose Really Necessary To God Or To Ourselves?

Another possible line of objection is to suggest that the quality (such as 'purpose giver') which the argument states is essential to God is not actually necessary to even a monotheistic God after all.

It is clearly true that we humans can exist without a purpose to life. After all there is no doubt that we humans (as indeed do animals and other life forms in the world) actually do exist and we exist irrespective of whether there is an ultimate purpose to life or not. Indeed for the most part we exist and continue with our lives without actually claiming to know of any purpose to our lives, or without even in general thinking too much about it. Of course it might well be useful if humans did have a sensible ultimate purpose and consequently a sense of direction. Yet I must agree that an ultimate purpose is evidently not an absolute necessity so far as we humans are concerned.

However in relation to a monotheistic God, purpose is more essential. God is never thought of as merely a great showman in the sky, a sort of superior kind of astronaut that created a great show of this world, just as adults might have put on a great fireworks display to impress their young children that was dazzling while it lasted but no more than that! If that was all there was to 'God' he would not be worthy, at least not morally worthy, of voluntary worship and sophisticated religions! So a monotheistic God to be worthy of the term 'God' must be more than a creative showman, more even than an omnipotent showman. So as a monotheistic God must be more than a mere creative showman he must therefore create with a constructive purpose in mind and must therefore infuse purpose into his creation and so into the Universe. Without a purpose infused creation our potential God can be no more than a great showman, albeit a very skilled showman but he cannot be a real monotheistic God. Therefore it is actually necessary for 'God' to give ultimate purpose to his world, his creation.

(iii) Can Providing A Purpose Be A Necessary Quality For God If It Is Logically Unachievable?

The objection here is that it can be argued that however desirable it may be for ultimate purpose to be given to life, it cannot logically be done and if it cannot be done God cannot do it – so it being impossible, it cannot be one of God's characteristic qualities. God is just maximally powerful but is not absolutely powerful beyond even the bounds of Logic. Furthermore it can be observed that the world actually gets along very nicely without overall ultimate purpose through a combination both of creatures having limited purposes such as making money or procreating and also by not thinking about such abstractions anyhow.

This I think is the strongest objection that can be put to the whole argument that the lack of ultimate purpose in the world is a reason why God does not exist. It is personally speaking why I prefer to argue for the non-existence of God from the impossibility of omniscience (which is a more demonstrably necessary quality for God) existing. Nevertheless it does remain true even if endowing ultimate purpose to anything is absolutely impossible that in the absence of purpose our Universe is merely a great show and its creator (or primary entity) is thereby a great showman and not a genuine monotheistic God. Of course I accept that limited or even false purposes such as an ultimately purposeless long line of procreation or making money or building empires can be effective (in human terms) substitutes for an ultimate purpose. I even accept that life without purpose is not merely possible but practicable – indeed one might be so busy or absorbed in life or even be so unquestioning about life that one never even notices the lack of overall purpose. Yet in the end if there is no purpose there can ultimately be no good and no bad ways to live life. Morality (or anything else) is then no longer underpinned and declines from being a principle to being at best a pragmatic way of avoiding difficulties with other people who seem to have at times strange and ultimately unjustifiable notions. In those circumstances 'God' too loses any element of moral support and becomes ultimately a powerful despot who cannot justify in moral terms his actions, his worship, his religions or even his own existence!

To me the questions of whether God can exist without having logically impossible characteristic qualities are questions of whether there are logically possible alternatives to any such qualities which are in effectiveness good enough. In the case of absolute omnipotence the replacement by 'maximal power' is to all practical intents and purposes good enough. However omniscience cannot be replaced by any good enough substitute short of omniscience because in the end knowledge is a nexus and one cannot risk operating with unknown gaps in knowledge – at an ultimate level knowledge must be complete or it risks being practically nothing. And in the case of endowing purpose because purpose is the only way that ultimately meaning and therefore ultimately morality can be endowed upon the world, genuine purpose cannot be substituted by a lesser quality to achieve the same genuine effect. So logically impossible or not it is absolutely essential that a monotheistic God does make the world ultimately purposeful. This is because if ultimate purpose cannot be bestowed upon the world, morality cannot be underpinned. As both the morality and the meaningfulness of God cannot in the absence of ultimate purpose be ultimately upheld, God cannot exist if he cannot bring ultimate purpose to the world. Therefore if it is asking the logically impossible (and I submit it is) for God to bring genuine meaning to the world and so indeed to himself one should conclude not that such a quality is unnecessary – it is ultimately necessary to a monotheistic God – but that the concept of God is even theoretically impossible and so God cannot exist.

(iv) Isn't Our Knowledge Too Limited To Know The Purpose Of Life?

The objection may be tried that there could well be an ultimate purpose to our lives and our world which we are unaware of since human knowledge is still too limited. Indeed some scientists are now claiming that the purpose (though I would not say ultimate purpose!) of our lives unbeknown at least to our conscious selves is not merely to procreate but in reality is to advance the chances of our own individual genes, our genetic material, in a competition for a dominant status in our world. So perhaps also unbeknown to us there could actually be a valid ultimate purpose to life.

Well maybe a genes-promotion purpose to life and maybe even some deeper purposes to life may in future be found to exist or even exist unfound. However in relation to our present argument and in relation to the possible existence of a monotheistic God unknown purposes of which we are ignorant are not good enough. For a start how can a purpose that is unknown to us while we live give any conscious meaning to our lives as we consciously live? And if we are unaware of it, what use could such a purpose be? Indeed for the most part such a purpose might as well not exist! Moreover purpose is important because of its relationship to morality but an unknown or unknowable purpose cannot affect morality nor underpin a moral dimension to life or existence, even a potential God's existence. Nor can an unknown purpose cause us to adjust our behaviour to accord with it. So in theological terms an unknown ultimate purpose to life is no use because it fails to either underpin morality or give meaning to those living life, both of which are primary functions of a monotheistic God in relation to purpose. The theological necessity for purpose is not the same as the scientific quest for discovery. In scientific terms what matters most of all is the sheer fact is there or is there not an ultimate purpose and whether we yet know about it is not necessarily of the greatest importance. However in theological terms what matters most of all is that an ultimate purpose if it exists exists to give morality and meaning to our lives which it cannot properly do if we do not know what such a purpose is. So in relation to this (theological) argument about the possible existence of God, God cannot properly have conferred purpose upon our world if we (who are living) do not know that purpose. This is because to get any benefit in terms of morality or meaning to life (which would be the essential concerns of a genuine God worthy of worship) we who live would have to actually know what that ultimate purpose is.

(v) Isn't There An Ultimate Purpose To Life If We Look For It?

It may be objected that so many different purposes to life have been put forward that the real difficulty should not be in finding any purpose to life but in finding the correct purpose among the many put forward. For instance many people suppose that procreation (i.e. having children) is the purpose of life and some scientists claim that perpetuating yourself through the spread of your genes is the purpose. Meanwhile moralists may claim that the purpose of life is 'to do good' and hedonists claim that the purpose of life is to enjoy oneself and religious theists tend to claim that the purpose of life is to worship and honour God.

That is indeed quite a selection of possible purposes (which incidentally can actually exist irrespective of whether God exists or not). However the problem with them all is though they may all be objectives in life none of them can amount to an ultimate purpose to life. Let us for instance consider procreation whether it be of children or of genes. I will mention in considering procreation the fact that in combining with one's partner to produce a child the result of the mixture of genes is a thorough dilution of your own genes. The resultant child is in many ways thoroughly unlike oneself and may indeed be distasteful to oneself. At any rate what a child is not in any real sense is a continuation of oneself – at most it ends up as being a continuation of a trace of oneself which of course is later further diluted if that child acquires a partner and has children! However even overlooking that, isn't it the case that everything, not only individuals but also races (like the dinosaurs, mammoths etc) and eventually even planets and stars all die in the end? So the prolongation of one's race into further generations does not answer the question of what is the ultimate purpose of it all either for individuals or even when considered collectively for races! Furthermore you can regress the question apparently infinitely – if you think you have found a purpose what ultimately is the purpose of that purpose? For instance if you claim the purpose of life is to enjoy oneself while one can, what ultimately is the purpose of that pleasure? After all it hardly seems to matter when you are dead or from the perspective of all eternity whether you enjoyed yourself or not. And as for doing good deeds or its variant of gaining access to Heaven through a virtuous life (apart from making up for a little of a supposed God's failure to organise the world beneficently for many people) what ultimate purpose does that fulfil? All these things, procreation, pleasure seeking or 'doing good' may pass the time of day and serve as one's objectives in life but none of them can ultimately be the result of the infusion of overall purpose into the Universe. They all ultimately lead to no final purpose that can demonstrate meaning in the Universe as a whole and through that provide ultimate meaning to one's own temporary part of the Universe, one's own life. Nor can the commonest and most orthodox monotheistic answer to what is the purpose of life, namely 'to worship and honour God' do any better in ultimate terms. The only difference to most of the other proffered purposes to life is that instead of leading to a regression of purposes and no ultimate purpose, it tends to lead to a meaningless circularity of purpose (i.e. 'The purpose of life is to honour God' and 'The purpose of honouring God is to fulfil one's purpose in life') but to no ultimate purpose that is intelligible, meaningful and unregressible.

So therefore although we can find possible tactical objectives or shorter term purposes in life it is impossible to find any ultimate or absolute purpose that is valid in terms of the Universe as a whole, or even ultimately valid in terms of our own selves.

So I can fairly state that none of these five possible lines of objection is able to invalidate the argument that God cannot exist because some of his essential qualities cannot exist (with particular reference to his role as 'our purpose giver'). Indeed the most that can be said for the best of these objections is that they may provoke one to think more deeply about the subject because that deeper thought may be necessary to reveal their fallacies. Therefore the argument that God cannot exist because some of God's essential qualities (including the quality of being 'the purpose giver' to the world) are not possible is still valid even after examining the objections that may most obviously be raised about the argument.

E. The Argument In Perspective

The argument that God cannot exist because some of his essential qualities cannot exist is basically a purist, logical argument against the existence of God. The first step is to determine what God's essential qualities would be – and God must indeed have some such qualities, otherwise he would not be distinctive nor identifiable. The second step is to analyse those qualities with a view to working out whether it is even possible for any entity to have such qualities. Then one can determine whether the very notion of God is paradoxical with God needing qualities that cannot exist in practice or alternatively whether God's existence is feasible, albeit unproven. This is a methodologically sound approach. However it does require the utmost care. First, one must carefully select which, if any, qualities are really absolutely essential to God (qualities that are objectively essential and not just convenient or seemingly likely). Secondly, one must analyse carefully the logically necessary (and not just the probable) consequences of those qualities. Finally, one must be very careful in analysing whether the quality itself is actually logically impossible rather than merely improbable or implausible.

Considered in relation to a potential monotheistic God's quality of being 'our purpose giver' the requirements are first to demonstrate that it is necessary for God to be our purpose giver and secondly then to prove that it is impossible for anything (including a potential God) to be our purpose giver in a real, absolute sense. If we can succeed in this then this argument is an absolute disproof of the existence of a monotheistic God. Although many philosophers have not included 'purpose giver' as a specific quality God requires, I contend that the quality of infusing purpose into the Universe is essential to God. It is absolutely necessary so as to underpin ultimate meaning and morality in the Universe, there being no other conceivable way of achieving that. In the absence of some ultimate purpose a great power, a daemon, may indeed exist and have created us but a monotheistic God (that necessarily has dimensions of ultimate meaningfulness and morality as well as sheer power) cannot ultimately exist. I reject the notion that an artificial goal or a practical set of purposes is an adequate substitute for a real ultimate, overall purpose because an artificial purpose is or potentially is transparent and is therefore ultimately insufficient to underpin morality and meaning in the world. On the second requirement that it is theoretically impossible to infuse ultimate purpose into the Universe, I assert that for moral and theological purposes it is sufficient to realise that we know of no ultimate purpose. So far as we are concerned there is no ultimate purpose because it is impossible for us to react to or even benefit consciously from purpose in our world if we ourselves know of no real purpose. Furthermore it is indeed impossible even to conceive of a real and final purpose to our world (that withstands critical examination).

So the argument that God cannot exist because his qualities cannot exist does work as a valid disproof of the existence of God in relation to the quality of his being our purpose giver. It does not work in relation to the qualities of God being eternal, omnipresent, consciously controlling and our ultimate creator because so far as I can see these are at least hypothetically possible qualities. It works in the case of literal omnipotence but not in the case of omnipotence modified into 'maximal power' to take account of Logic. It works in the case of 'supreme goodness' because the concept itself is subjective and is linguistically a confused amalgam but it may be possible to amend this particular quality to take account of these problems. (However what any feasible amendment pretty certainly cannot take account of is the fact that the world we live in is clearly not the product of anything like supreme goodness in its creation but that is another argument!) The argument also works very well in the case of omniscience as omniscience is demonstrably an essential quality of God and it is also demonstrably a quality that cannot be attained.

So in conclusion this argument that God cannot exist because his qualities cannot exist can lead to absolute and logical disproofs of the existence of God. Furthermore this argument does actually lead at least in relation to some qualities to logical and absolute disproofs of the existence of a monotheistic God.

Conclusion

In this book I have provided six arguments why nobody can logically believe in the existence of a monotheistic God. I have been proving beyond conceivable doubt that God cannot exist (and certainly cannot exist in any worthwhile, worth praying to form). My method has been to apply the same logic to this problem as we would gladly have applied to other things. Indeed I have been even more rigorous than the British legal standard of criminal proof of 'beyond reasonable doubt' since I think that God can be proved not to exist 'beyond conceivable doubt'. So far as I know the six arguments I have presented are all at least in part (and sometimes in their entirety) original arguments. Yet they are all logically valid arguments in relation to monotheism.

In relation to polytheism which I have not considered in detail in this book only some of these arguments apply. Yet sufficient logical arguments do apply to polytheism to prove that all polytheistic religions are irrational, wrong and contrary to Logic and should not be believed in by anybody.

Briefly, not all my arguments apply to polytheism since the claims in terms of absolute qualities of polytheistic Gods are more modest than in monotheism (so much so as to make polytheistic 'Gods' fundamentally different in kind to any monotheistic 'God'). The argument that 'God Has No Explanatory Value' does not apply because polytheistic Gods do not claim very much in the way of ultimate explanatory value. Nor does 'The Aggregate Of Qualities Argument' apply because there are hardly sufficient absolute qualities to aggregate. The 'This Is Not The Best Possible World Argument' does not apply since polytheistic religions generally do not endow the combination of supreme goodness and omnipotence on any of their gods. The 'Some Of God's Defining Qualities Cannot Exist Argument' applies only in part to polytheism. It applies for instance in relation to any claims by or on behalf of polytheistic Gods that they can be sure of being immortal. However it does not apply to some other qualities (such as being 'the purpose giver' to the Universe) which polytheistic 'Gods' do not claim to have and need not necessarily have.

Other arguments certainly do apply to polytheism. The 'God Is Many Sided Argument' and the 'Time And Space Argument' (both of which I outlined in the Introduction) are applicable. Both apply in relation to the sheer improbability, the infinitesimal, in effect the zero chance of any of the almost innumerable differing versions of polytheism being true. Also valid in relation to polytheism are the arguments relating to the absolute unidentifiability of Gods either by humans or even by themselves. Neither humans nor even the supposed polytheistic Gods themselves can have any infallible means of knowing for certain that they are immortal into all the future (which has not and never will have all occurred). Nor can any entity, including themselves, actually be certain that they really have full power or control even of their own, albeit limited, supposed sphere of power (be it the oceans in the case of the ancient Roman God, Neptune, or be it destruction in the case of the Hindu God, Siva). Such candidate polytheistic Gods (if such hypothetically existed) might believe they have such power and are immortal but there is no logically valid means of verifying or properly 'knowing' those things. Indeed such characteristics are ultimately incapable of being positively identified. So neither finite mortal humans nor even supposed polytheistic Gods themselves can be certain anything, including themselves, are genuinely either immortal for all time into the future or are ultimately fully supreme over any aspect of our world. Therefore 'The Man And God Comprehension Gulf Argument' and 'The Universal Uncertainty Argument' are both ultimately just as applicable in relation to logically disproving polytheistic claims as monotheistic claims.

Perhaps there are yet more atheistical arguments still to be found. However I hope before too long the consensus of opinion will be that there is no need to find yet more valid arguments against God's existence because it will become a generally accepted fact that God cannot exist. I hope it will soon be generally accepted that a rational approach proves that the concept of God is like a fairy tale that is untrue and indeed in the case of God logically incapable of being true. Therefore in seeking an explanation of how we humans and the Universe came to exist it will then be understood that creation by a monotheistic (i.e. omnipotent, omniscient, eternal and perfectly good etc) God is not logically possible. We must therefore consider other possible explanations as the 'God' theory is wrong, indeed impossible in Logic. Perhaps in the end I will even be credited with helping to destroy belief in the concept of God through putting forward these logical proofs that God should not be believed in.

So I maintain it is contrary to Logic and absurd to actually believe in a religion. Of course this is running into direct conflict with 'faith' but I do so boldly and unrepentantly. It is now fashionable for religions to talk about 'faith' which encourages religious people to say – 'I cannot prove I am right but I have faith there is a God. You can't prove my faith is wrong and there isn't a God. So as that is the case I will arbitrarily believe that I am right and act accordingly.' This misses the point. Without evidence it is plain wrong to believe in anything – it is correct to proceed believing in nothing. I do not believe in invisible pink elephants without (or against) evidence. If I did everybody would think it absurd. Even more so if I collected food for the invisible pink elephants. Nor for that matter am I actively not believing in invisible pink elephants. I am just taking the situation as it comes as in law where guilt is not believed in unless it can be proved beyond reasonable doubt, which religions manifestly have not done with God. The introduction of the concept of 'faith' is an admission of that. This principle of non-belief in what is not evidenced should be even stronger, indeed absolute, in any instances (as with God) where the hypothecated phenomenon is not merely insufficiently evidenced but where it is actually contrary to Logic and so contrary to reason for such a phenomenon to exist. Yet somehow as a society we are not being logical nor even sensible about religion – to use my analogy we are putting out food for the invisible pink elephants. Some might argue that religion is too important a matter to be indifferent about. I have argued that God's existence would actually be contrary to Logic and therefore inconceivable but anyhow even in the absence of clear knowledge it would be ridiculous to act as if we knew God exists. Moreover by following religions people are betraying truth and doing so without justification. By rejecting religions we would be respecting truth – surely the basis of our advanced civilisation. So I urge people to stop accepting our religious traditions unquestioningly on trust or faith and start reconsidering them as I have done here.

Of course it is not absolutely impossible (though I personally doubt it) that some creator of ourselves, or very powerful daemon may exist and exercise control over our part of the Universe. However, as I have proved, such a creator daemon cannot genuinely be God (as this is not the best possible world and even it, the creating daemon, cannot possibly be sure of its own mortality or its own relationship to the Universe as a whole). Furthermore that creator daemon (if he existed) if he is indeed 'good' would not mind if we do not believe in God's existence, especially as neither we nor even he could logically believe in the existence of God. He would surely then be prepared to judge us (if he judges at all) by the 'good' that we do according to the reasonable standards of our environment, our intellect and Logic. Men's worth cannot fairly be judged by whether they believe in invisible pink elephants or irrational religions or not. People may – though I don't know – be expected to do 'good'. People cannot reasonably be expected to abandon the standard of adhering as closely as possible to perceived truth on which they depend for a livelihood in other things but without any logical reason break away from it in religion. No reasonable daemon could expect it. And if this hypothetical daemon is not reasonable, then powerful as it may be, there is certainly no moral value in worshipping it or 'God'. It is – and may it long continue to be so – a great principle of mankind that men do not voluntarily revere naked power but moral greatness alone. So if a powerful daemon (which is the nearest thing to God that could, unlikely though it may be, within the bounds of Logic exist) exists, and if it were worth worshipping, it would understand why we cannot reasonably worship it as God – otherwise it should not be voluntarily worshipped because powerful as it may be, it is not worthy of voluntary worship.

In this book I have denounced The Comprehension Paradox (and by implication those, such as theists who gratuitously believe things in accordance with it), namely

'– God is beyond human comprehension.
– I comprehend that it is God that exists.'

I have uncompromisingly dared to continue questioning and penetrating the realities of religious belief in areas where we, mere mortals, are not supposed by religions to probe. I have done this in the mortal belief that nothing but true, direct answers (and these only sometimes) should stop us from reiterating our questions. I have done this in the belief that details are to be examined and penetrated whatever. In short I have done this in the name of reason. I proclaim that the case of reason (rationality) ought to be put in cosmological and indeed in political, ethical, scientific and all other terms. To depart from (or 'transcend') reason is to ignore the foundations on which we have built up our civilisation and will, wherever it is done, end in unreality and abject failure. Those who believe in the irrational, whether it be in irrational, invisible pink elephants or in the existence of a monotheistic God that is contrary to Logic, deserve to be ridiculed as we necessarily must live by the rational. Neither we nor anything else (including even any potential God) could by definition understand or even cope with the irrational since the irrational is necessarily unpredictable and ultimately unknowable. So I have to the best of my ability put the case of reason. That case disproves the existence of God. I have achieved all that I wish to achieve in this book if I have made it logically clear that the existence of God would be contrary to Logic. The concept of a monotheistic God cannot be reconciled with Logic and 'reason', reason by which we all must live.

Summaries of the Six Arguments – The Six Ways of Atheism

The Aggregate of Qualities Argument

1. If God exists, God must necessarily possess all of several remarkable qualities (including supreme goodness, omnipotence, immortality, omniscience, ultimate creator, purpose giver).

2. Every one of these qualities may not exist in any one entity and if any such quality does exist it exists in few entities or in some cases (e.g. omnipotence, ultimate creator) in at most one entity.

3. Therefore it is highly unlikely any entity would possess even one of these qualities.

4. There is an infinitesimal chance that any one entity (given the almost infinite number of entities in the Universe) might possess the combination of even some two of these qualities, let alone all of them.

5. In statistical analysis a merely hypothetical infinitesimal chance can in effect be treated as the no chance to which it approximates so very closely.

6. Therefore as there is statistically such an infinitesimal chance of any entity possessing, as God would have to do, all God's essential qualities in combination it can be said for all practical and statistical purposes that God just does not exist.

The Man And God Comprehension Gulf Argument

1. Man is finite (in time, space and power etc).

2. God if he exists is infinite (in time, space and power etc).

3. Therefore mankind cannot possibly recognise God or even know that God exists.

The 'God Has No Explanatory Value' Argument

1. God if he exists must be the ultimate being and provide the answer to all our ultimate questions – otherwise he is not really God.

2. Yet even supposing as a hypothesis that God exists the questions that God was supposed to finally answer still remain (though in some cases God is substituted in the question for the Universe).

3. Therefore hypothesising God's existence is only unnecessarily adding an extra stage to such problems and has no real explanatory value.

4. Therefore according to Logic (Occam's Razor Law – 'that entities are not to be multiplied beyond necessity') we should not postulate God's existence and there is no adequate reason to suppose that God exists.

5. Therefore we should suppose that God does not exist.

The 'This Is Not The Best Possible World' Argument

1. God if he exists must be omnipotent, supremely good and our ultimate creator.

2. Therefore an existent God (being supremely good and competent) would have created the best possible world (if he created anything).

3. As the world is inconsistent (between ages and people) it cannot all be the best possible world.

4. Therefore as the world is not the best possible world, God cannot exist.

The Universal Uncertainty Argument

1. An uncertain God is a contradiction in terms.

2. Everything in the Universe must be fundamentally uncertain about its own relationship to the Universe as a whole because there is no way of attaining such certainty.

3. Therefore even an entity with all God's other qualities cannot have the final quality of certain knowledge concerning its own relationship to the Universe as a whole.

4. Therefore God cannot exist because even any potential God cannot know for sure that it is God.

Note: Stated as a logical paradox this argument is 'God cannot exist because God cannot know for sure that it is God'.

The 'Some Of God's Defining Qualities Cannot Exist' Argument

1. God must have certain characteristic qualities (such as providing purpose to life), otherwise he would not be God.

2. But it is impossible for any entity to possess some of these qualities (such as providing purpose to life since we can find no real purpose and therefore we in practice have no ultimate purpose to our lives) that are essential to God.

3. Therefore since some of God's essential qualities (such as being the purpose provider to life) cannot possibly exist in any entity, God cannot exist.